INTERNATIONAL BOND ISSUES OF THE
LESS-DEVELOPED COUNTRIES: DIAGNOSIS AND PRESCRIPTION

INTERNATIONAL BOND ISSUES

OF THE LESS-DEVELOPED COUNTRIES:
Diagnosis and Prescription

HANG-SHENG CHENG

The Iowa State University Press,

AMES, IOWA

HANG-SHENG CHENG, Associate Professor of Economics, Iowa State University, came to Iowa State in 1963 upon receiving the Ph.D. degree from Princeton University. Prior to his studies at Princeton, he was for ten years (1951–1961) a member of the research staff of the International Monetary Fund. He also holds the B.A. degree from Tsing Hwa University, Peiping, China, the M.A. degree from George Washington University, and did graduate work at Johns Hopkins University. During the academic year of 1968–1969, he was on leave from Iowa State University to serve on an assignment for the Asia Foundation as an Adviser to the Commission on Taxation Reform of the Republic of China and as the Chief of the Commission's First Division in charge of economic analysis. Besides this book, his writings include articles and reviews published in *The American Economic Review, The Southern Economic Journal,* and *The International Monetary Fund Staff Papers.*

© 1969 The Iowa State University Press
Ames, Iowa, U.S.A. All rights reserved

Composed and printed by
The Iowa State University Press

First edition, 1969

Standard Book Number: 8138–1679–3
Library of Congress Catalog Card Number: 69–18486

TO MY DEAR WIFE, SHING

PREFACE

THIS BOOK seeks to answer two questions: First, why have the international bond issues of the less-developed countries since the end of the Second World War been so small both in absolute amounts and by comparison with their volumes in the 1920's? And second, what can be done to help bring about a vigorous revival of the international market for these issues and at the same time to provide a safeguard against recurrences of the ills that so plagued the market in the past?

To some, the first question may seem hardly worth asking. Anyone at all acquainted with the developments in international finance during the last forty years can point to: the bitter experiences of widespread foreign-bond defaults in the 1930's, the political and economic instability in many of the less-developed countries since the end of the Second World War, and the heavy burden of external debt these countries are already carrying, as familiar and obvious answers to that question.

However, as I hope I have demonstrated in Chapter 3, none of these familiar and seemingly obvious answers stands up well under close scrutiny. Like most glib answers to an inherently difficult question, each of them contains some elements of plausibility, but fails to hold up when countered by substantial evidence. The superficiality of these answers contributes to their popularity, and their unquestioned acceptance by many preempts the will to search for the conditions needed to restore a viable and stable international capital market. Chapter 3 is devoted, therefore, to an iconoclastic task of deflating these popular beliefs so as to clear the way for a fresh outlook on the question.

As I approached the first question, it seemed to me that any acceptable answer must account for the essential differences between the conditions prevailing prior to 1914 and during the 1920's, which enabled the international security markets to serve as a major source of development finance, and those prevailing since 1930, which have evidently prevented these markets from resuming their former role. The thought led me to suspect that a stable international capital market must be anchored to a smoothly functioning international monetary system. The hypothesis seems to agree well with the observation that the gradual reactivation of the international capital market for the securities of the developed countries paralleled the rise of an emerging new international monetary order among those countries; whereas, in contrast, the great majority of the less-developed countries have taken no part in that emerging international monetary order and at the same time have been virtually excluded from participating in the rising international capital market among the developed countries. Chapter 4, devoted to the development and elaboration of this theme, should be of interest not only to those whose primary concern rests with international capital markets, but also to those interested in the broader problem of the future of the international monetary system.

In some respects, Chapter 5 may appear as a digression, but in fact the topic it deals with is closely related to the second question this book seeks to answer concerning the means to help bring about a sustainable revival of the international market for the less-developed countries' bond issues. It examines, then rejects, the World Bank's official explanations for its failure to use the authority granted to it by its Articles of Agreement to provide guarantees to its member countries' security issues in international capital markets. Instead, it suggests that the use of the World Bank's guarantee authority is perhaps precluded by the logic inherent in its Articles of Agreement, a point which may have escaped the notice of the Bank's founding fathers and becomes clear only in the light of the Bank's subsequent operating experiences.

On the basis of the observations made in Chapter 4, the final chapter of this book outlines a proposal for the establishment of a scheme whereby the World Bank could issue "certifications" of its less-developed members' international bond issues. Although the basic idea underlying the scheme may appear unfamiliar in the international sphere, its workability has in fact been tested out in the domestic spheres of countries with stable and vigorous domestic capital markets. Its principal features may be regarded as a cross between the registration requirements of the U.S. Securities and Exchange Commission on the one hand and the bank-examination requirement and liquidity bailout facilities of the U.S. Federal Reserve System on the other. Its intent is to help breathe new life into the international capital market for the less-developed countries' security issues without undermining its essential private-investment nature. In other words, it seeks to reduce the extent of the incalculable political risks which private investors cannot be expected to undertake, but it in no way attempts to shift risk-taking from the private to the public domain.

Whether the proposed scheme is feasible and efficacious is of course open to serious questions. I aspire to no more than offering it as a possible starting point for discussion by all who are concerned with the present dim prospect for substantially enlarging the flow of financial resources to the less-developed countries despite general professions of such a need. From a historical viewpoint, if private investment can be considered as the "engine of economic growth" during the nineteenth century, the international security market was no doubt the principal pipeline through which flowed the indispensable fuel. Now that the line has largely run dry, a concentrated effort must be made to explore all possible means to get the flow restarted in a volume commensurate with the need.

H. S. CHENG

Taipei, Taiwan
September 1968

ACKNOWLEDGMENTS

IN THE PREPARATION of this book, I have been aided by numerous persons to whom I am much indebted. Edgar R. Koerner, Kuhn, Loeb and Co., New York; Samuel Pizer, formerly of the U.S. Department of Commerce; and Arthur E. Tiemann, World Bank, provided many of the unpublished data used. Burton G. Malkiel, Princeton University, and Robert J. Beh, Carleton D. Beh Co., Des Moines, Iowa, helped me to solve a number of technical difficulties in deriving the security-yield data used in Chapter 3. Arthur L. Wadsworth, Dillon, Read and Co., New York; Dale R. Weigel, U.S. Agency for International Development; and Edmund H. Worthy, U.S. Securities and Exchange Commission, sent me much-needed information at an early stage in preparation.

In December, 1967, I visited the World Bank in Washington, D.C., and benefited greatly from informal discussions with John H. Adler, Dragoslav Avramovic, and Mrs. Shirley Boskey of the Bank's staff. Later, copies of a draft of this book were sent to numerous leading figures in international finance, and many of them were kind enough to respond. I am especially grateful for the helpful comments of Richard H. Demuth and Irving S. Friedman of the World Bank; Jacques J. Polak of the International Monetary Fund; U.S. Senators Jacob K. Javits and Jack Miller; David Horowitz of the Bank of Israel; Nien-Tzu Wang of the U.N. Secretariat; Guy F. Erb of the UNCTAD's New York office; Arnold W. Sametz, New York University, and Harold T. Shapiro, University of Michigan.

Above all, I am indebted to Karl A. Fox, Head, Department of Economics, Iowa State University, for giving an extraordinary amount of his time, interest, assistance, and encouragement to this study. Not only did he read through the entire text of an earlier draft and make numerous helpful suggestions for its improvement, but he also undertook the laborious task of seeing the final manuscript through the press while I was on leave from the university.

Mrs. Rita Bauman typed the manuscript. Mrs. Charlotte Latta supervised the preparation of statistical data in several of the tables.

To all the above persons, I am sincerely grateful, although I alone am responsible for errors that may yet remain.

H. S. CHENG

CONTENTS

xiii

INTERNATIONAL BOND ISSUES OF THE
LESS-DEVELOPED COUNTRIES: DIAGNOSIS AND PRESCRIPTION

CHAPTER ONE

INTRODUCTION AND SUMMARY

AMONG THOSE CONCERNED with economic development of the less-developed countries a consensus now prevails that the flow of financial resources from the developed to the less-developed countries needs to be substantially expanded. In view of the increasing difficulty in persuading national legislatures of major donor countries to augment their appropriations for foreign-aid programs, thoughts naturally turn to possible means of expanding *private* capital flows to the less-developed countries. One such means, frequently suggested lately, is through direct security issues by these countries in international capital markets.

From hindsight, it is indeed surprising that until recently so little consideration had been given to this possibility since the establishment of the Bretton Woods institutions. After all, throughout the nineteenth century, international security markets, especially the London market, played a key role in the financing of economic development of the then developing nations. After World War

4   I, the mantle of international development finance passed to the New York capital market. During the decade of the 1920's, *public* issues of the less-developed countries in the United States alone amounted to more than $2.8 billion, attaining an average volume of about $440 million a year during the boom of the U.S. security market from 1926 to 1928. In contrast, the *total* issues, including both public and private issues, of the less-developed countries in the United States after World War II amounted to only $45 million in the first postwar decade 1946–55 and $612 million in the second postwar decade 1956–65.[1] Since in the meantime, from the late 1920's to the mid-1960's, prices in the United States approximately doubled, the size of the U.S. new-issue market quadrupled, and the U.S. gross national product increased by more than six-fold, the decline in the volume of the less-developed countries' issues in the U.S. market has indeed been exceedingly steep both in real terms and in relation to the size of that market. The sharp decline bespeaks on the one hand the difficulty of the less-developed countries' returning to the market under the present circumstances, and on the other the vast untapped potential that lies ahead, if only these countries can be assisted to regain a good portion of their former shares in the U.S. (and other) international issues markets as in the 1920's.

Tantalizing as the idea may be, the prospect of its realization in the near future is generally conceded to be quite limited. The consensus of careful analysts of the problem[2] is that, in view of: the poor credit standing of the less-developed countries and the high costs of borrowing in international capital markets; the heavy burden of external debts many of these countries are already carry-

---

[1] Not including Israeli issues.

[2] See, for instance, International Bank for Reconstruction and Development, *Annual Report 1966–1967,* pp. 35–38; International Monetary Fund, *1967 Annual Report,* pp. 32–38; United Nations, Department of Economic and Social Affairs, *World Economic Survey, 1965* (New York, 1966), pp. 48–57.

ing; and the restrictions on foreign issues in some European markets; a substantial expansion in the volume of the less-developed countries' external issues is highly unlikely in the near future.

Without disputing the soundness of this judgment, one may nevertheless offer the following two observations: first, an in-depth study is needed to look into the basic causes of the less-developed countries' failure to make effective use of international security markets since the 1920's; one suspects that some of the usual explanations refer to *symptoms* rather than *sources* of the problem. Second, suggestions of positive measures are needed to reactivate international security markets as a major source of capital for economic development and to build into the market mechanism safeguards effective enough to prevent recurrent confidence crises that have seriously disrupted the capital flows through these markets in the past. This essay is intended as a contribution toward fulfilling these needs.

In Chapter 2, I will present data on the volume of the less-developed countries' recent issues in various international capital markets. I will then take a close look at the volume of such issues in the U.S. market in particular, in order to bring into sharper focus the ebb and flow of such issues in that important market since 1920, with special emphasis on the developments during the two postwar decades from 1946 through 1965.

In Chapter 3, a thorough examination is made of several factors which have often been cited as "explanations" for the less-developed countries' failure to borrow in international security markets. Specifically, they are (1) debt record, (2) political instability, (3) existing external-debt burden, (4) costs of borrowing, and (5) legal and administrative hurdles. Each of these factors is carefully sifted so as to separate "basic factors" from mere myths with regard to the problem at hand.

6   On the basis of the analysis presented in Section 3, I evaluate in Section 4 the prospect of the less-developed countries' new issues in the U.S. and other international capital markets. Obviously, generalizations on this matter cannot be very helpful. For a number of less-developed countries, where conditions are favorable, there should not be much difficulty in doubling or even tripling their present total volume of issues in the near future, especially if a technical-assistance program could be instituted under the auspices of the investment-banking industries to facilitate the legal, administrative, and marketing process of issuing securities in these markets. For the majority of the less-developed countries, however, improving the efficiency of the international security markets would not suffice. Furthermore, even for the more favorably situated less-developed countries, although private capital flows to them could be substantially expanded in the short run, there is little assurance that the flows would not be abruptly cut off during times of confidence crisis, resulting in severe losses to the investors and extreme stringency to the debtor countries.

A brief survey of the developments in the international security markets since the nineteenth century suggests two basic factors which might account for the failure of these markets in the last almost forty years to resume their former role as a major source for development finance: (1) incalculability of risks from private investors' viewpoint of investment in less-developed countries' securities because of the large dependence of these countries' debt-servicing capacities on government policies in these countries on the one hand and on the policy decisions of the developed nations and of various public international agencies on the other; and (2) the lack of a smoothly functioning international monetary order linking the less-developed countries with the developed countries that would reduce to a minimum the "transfer problem" between them. Essential conditions for such an international monetary order to prevail include (a) ample provision of international liquidity to absorb temporary disturbances to external-payments positions, and (b) harmonization of economic policies that would permit and expedite effective real adjustments for the elimination of persistent payments imbalances. Developments in the last decade or so indicate that such an international monetary order has been emerging among the developed nations with few, if any, of the less-developed countries participating in that rising new monetary order. The nonfulfillment of these basic conditions with respect to the less-developed countries means that unless positive measures are taken to ameliorate the situation, the prospect of a sustained growth in their security issues in international markets is very dim indeed.

The need for massive public assistance to foster private capital flows to war-devastated and developing nations in the postwar years was clearly foreseen by the founding fathers of the Bretton Woods system. The scheme they proposed for meeting this need was written into the Articles of Agreement of the International Bank for Reconstruction and Development, providing the Bank with an authority to issue guarantees on its members' securities floated in international markets. The authority, however, has never been used by the Bank. Chapter 5 probes into the reasons for the Bank's not using that authority and attributes it to the logic inherent in the mode of operation prescribed by its Articles of Agreement. From hindsight, it seems obvious that the use of the guarantee power would be neither necessary nor desirable in view of other superior methods open to the Bank of generating private capital flows to the less-developed countries.

Yet the need for assisting the less-developed countries' security flotations in international markets stands unfulfilled. Since there appears to be little reason for the Bank to exercise its guarantee power in the foreseeable

8 future, an alternative scheme is needed to take the place of the Bank-guarantee scheme which in fact has never worked.

The scheme proposed in Chapter 6 calls on the Bank to undertake certification of less-developed countries' bond issues in international markets upon the borrowing country's request, and upon satisfaction also of a number of specified conditions. A "World Bank certification" would be a formal proclamation by the Bank that it has examined and found satisfactory the borrower's ability to service the new debt in accordance with the terms set forth in the bond issues, and that the Bank further commits itself to take an active interest in the continued observance of these terms throughout the life of the issue.

Specifically, the scheme envisages (1) that the Bank and the borrowing country reach an understanding concerning the intended use of the net proceeds of the issue in the framework of the borrowing country's development program, and on the projected policy measures for implementing the development program and maintaining a viable balance-of-payments position; (2) subsequent periodical reviews of the country's economic condition and policies to insure the country's continued ability to meet its external obligations; (3) a commitment on the part of the borrowing country to consider submitting future disputes concerning the Bank-certified bonds for conciliation and arbitration to the International Centre for Settlement of Investment Disputes; and (4) that either the borrowing country becomes eligible for emergency assistance under the proposed Supplementary Financial Measures scheme now under consideration by the United Nations Conference on Trade and Development[3] or that the Bank will undertake to organize consultative groups of capital-exporting nations to provide financial assistance during times

[3] See **IBRD**, *Supplementary Financial Measures* (Washington, December 1965).

of unexpected stress in the borrowing country's external payments.

These measures are believed to be efficacious and sufficient to remove the major obstacles to the less-developed countries' issuing securities in international markets and provide the basis that is presently lacking for a sustained growth in these issues.

What is suggested above should be perfectly in line with the current trend of rising demand for more coordination of international aid to the less-developed countries.[4] The multiplicity of national and international agencies for channeling financial and technical resources to the less-developed countries, each agency having its own procedures and requirements and often working at cross purposes with or in duplication of others, has been a source of wasted effort and funds for the aid-giving countries and of baffling administrative burdens for the countries receiving aid. Insofar as the bond-certification scheme proposed in this study envisions a more extensive use of the aid-consortia, aid-consultative groups or some other variant technique of international-aid coordination, its adoption and successful operation should help to shift the mode of operation in the field of international aid to the less-developed countries toward a greater degree of order and rationality than has hitherto existed.

Desirable as the goal may be, progress toward it is likely to be slow, intermittent, and at times imperceptible. In view of the vigilance with which national governments and international agencies keep guard over what they consider as prerogatives and established ways of operation, realism dictates that the bond-certification scheme proposed in this study innovate in a way which would require minimal break with what has been familiar and accepted. As will be explained more fully in Chapter 6, the pre-cer-

[4] See U.N. *World Economic Survey, 1965*, pp. 131–38; and the proposed supplementary financial measures scheme cited in the preceding footnote.

10 tification investigation and the post-certification consultations envisaged in the scheme are what the World Bank has been doing all along in administering its own loans to its member countries; similarly, the commitment to submit to conciliation or arbitration procedures of the International Centre for Settlement of Investment Disputes and the recourse to emergency assistance through aid-consultative groups are both building on existing planks. Even the central idea of the scheme—opening up the World Bank's incomparable wealth of information for, and experience in, evaluating the long-run economic prospects of its member countries and putting it to use for assisting private investors' appraisal of the creditworthiness of the less-developed countries' international bond issues— is merely an extension of what the World Bank has for years been doing in joint loan operations with private investment banks.[5] What is new, however, is the recombination of familiar elements in a new framework for a new purpose: the rejuvenation of the international market for the less-developed countries' bond issues.

Inevitably, the question is to be asked: What if a borrowing country defaults on its Bank-certified bonds? The answer to that is: nothing; that is, nothing beyond what is outlined above. The purpose of the scheme is to encourage private capital flows to the less-developed countries, not to substitute for such flows. In a sense, a private capital flow that carries a full-fledged public guarantee is

[5] In a private communication to the author, a high official of the World Bank pointed out: "In those cases where we believe developing countries have sufficient credit worthiness to justify the sale of their bonds in the private market, but where the market may be reluctant for reasons of unfamiliarity or otherwise to accept them, we have sometimes organized a financing transaction under which a portion of the country's financial requirements is met by a Bank loan and the remaining requirements are met by a concurrent public offering or private placement of bonds in the market, often for the same project as that for which the Bank loan is made. In a theoretical model the Bank would take the larger share of the financing at first and the market a much smaller portion, but gradually, as the market became familiar with the country's paper, the proportions would shift and eventually we would try to get the country in such a strong position that there was no longer need for Bank help."

no longer a private investment—functionally, it is no different from lending the funds to the guaranteeing institution to enable the latter to relend the proceeds to the ultimate borrower; the essential risk-taking function of private investment is thereby emasculated. In contrast, the scheme proposed in this study purports to advise and facilitate private risk-taking so as to assist the market to stand on its own, not to be upholding it all the time.

Two questions might arise at this point. First, would the World Bank still feel "morally responsible" for the bonds it had certified even though no guarantee were to be explicitly stated in the certification? Second, would private capital be forthcoming in volume without the Bank's guarantee?

In answer to the first question, all the Bank's responsibilities, moral or otherwise, must be explicitly stated and understood by all parties concerned. The World Bank should be no more responsible for possible defaults of the bonds it certifies than the Federal Reserve System of the United States for possible bankruptcies of the banks it examines. To insist on the World Bank's taking on more responsibilities than that would be analogous to insisting that courts of law make good the losses from burglaries that law-enforcement authorities have failed to prevent.

As to the second question, the answer is an emphatic *Yes*. Under the scheme, private capital would be forthcoming without formal or informal guarantees by the World Bank. The rest of this study is mostly devoted to a substantiation of this answer. Nevertheless, three brief remarks may be in order here:

(1) In the nearly quarter of a century since the end of World War II, foreign private investors have poured huge amounts of capital into the less-developed countries in forms of investment other than these countries' international bond issues. Most of these investments have been without recourse to any public guarantee schemes.

(2) During the same period, the less-developed countries have borrowed and fully serviced billions of dollars of foreign debts to private investment institutions as well as to public foreign-aid agencies. There is no reason to expect that this nearly perfect debt record cannot be kept up in the years to come.

(3) Under the scheme proposed in this study, both investors and borrowers would be aware that the World Bank would be working diligently to see to it that the terms of the bonds carrying its certification were observed in full. Any default of such bonds would in effect constitute an open flout of the authority and prestige of both the World Bank and the International Centre for Settlement of Investment Disputes. In John Maynard Keynes's words, used in a slightly different but entirely parallel situation, "(the) borrower will be under an overwhelming motive to do its best and play fair, for the consequences of improper action and avoidable default to so great an institution will not be lightly incurred."[6]

In conclusion, a momentous decision confronts the world today. The alternative to drifting through inaction or inadequate actions into a further widening of the gulf between the rich and the poor nations must be massive aid to help the latter nations to help themselves. To date, the United Nations Development Decade has failed to call forth a substantial increase in the volume of financial aid to the less-developed nations, mainly because it vainly pinned its hope on national legislatures to respond to the call and voluntarily increase appropriations for aid to the less-developed nations. Political reality has dashed that hope. At the same time, international new-issue markets, which played a key role in development finance in the nineteenth century, remain untapped. Of course, condi-

---

[6] See "Opening remarks of Lord Keynes at the first meeting of the Second Commission on the Bank for Reconstruction and Development" in *Proceedings and Documents of the United Nations Monetary and Financial Conference, Bretton Woods, New Hampshire, July 1–22, 1944* (Washington, D.C.: U.S. Department of State, 1948), I, 87.

tions have changed greatly since the nineteenth century. But, recognizing in what essential ways conditions have changed and on the basis of this recognition to suggest ways of re-establishing favorable conditions for the less-developed countries' international issues must be among the first steps toward restoring the international new-issue markets as a major source of development finance. In my estimation, feasible means for attaining this goal are at hand and the time is now ripe for bold actions to put these means to work, or at least to give serious consideration to their adoption. I hope this essay will help to stimulate thinking in that direction.

CHAPTER TWO

BOND ISSUES OF THE LESS-DEVELOPED COUNTRIES IN INTERNATIONAL CAPITAL MARKETS, 1920-1929 AND 1946-1966

MANY PEOPLE are aware that the less-developed countries have been unable to float bonds in quantity in the international capital markets since the end of the 1920's, but few know exactly how unsuccessful they have been. In recent years, through the efforts of the United Nations Secretariat and the World Bank staff, much information on these countries' bond issues in international capital markets has been compiled and published. In this chapter we examine the available data on the volumes of such issues in all major markets during the years 1952 through 1966, and then concentrate on the developments in the U.S. market in particular. In the latter market, because of the greater availability of data, we shall be able to compare the bond issues of the less-developed countries in the two postwar decades 1946–65 with those during the decade of the 1920's, and to present a more detailed analysis of the individual less-developed countries' issues during the postwar period.

For presentation of statistical data, the "less-developed countries" are defined in this paper to include all the countries and territories in Latin America and the Caribbean (other than Puerto Rico), Africa (other than the Union of South Africa), and Asia (other than Turkey, Cyprus, Israel, North Viet Nam, Mainland China, North Korea, and Japan).

Table 2.1 presents data on the total volumes of these countries' bond issues in five major international capital markets—New York, London, Geneva, Frankfurt, and Brussels—in the 15 years 1952 through 1966. During that period, the less-developed countries issued altogether $1.5 billion of bonds in the five markets. The average volume of about $100 million a year during that period was minute indeed compared to the annual average of $39 billion *total* new issues in the United States alone and of $2.7 billion *foreign* new issues in all major capital markets during the 1963–66 period.[7]

The data in Table 2.1 also indicate that, as far as bond issues of the less-developed countries are concerned, the New York market did not achieve its predominance until 1960. In the 1950's, few less-developed countries resorted to the New York market, and London was by far the largest market for the bond issues of those countries. Such issues in London, however, declined sharply after 1959, and except for a brief spurt in 1963,[8] London has not been an active market for the new issues of the less-developed countries. At about the same time, continental European capi-

[7] For the 1963–66 data, see *Federal Reserve Bulletin,* December 1967, p. 2114, and International Monetary Fund, *Annual Report, 1967,* p. 32.

[8] Two-thirds of the $39 million bonds of the less-developed countries issued in London in 1963 were accounted for by issues of Malaysia and Nigeria, $14 million and $12 million respectively. See United Nations, Department of Economic and Social Affairs, *World Economic Survey, 1965* (New York, 1966), pp. 51–52.

TABLE 2.1. Bond Issues of the Less-developed Countries in International Capital Markets, 1952–66

Year	All Markets	New York	London	Geneva	Frankfurt	Brussels
	(millions of dollars)					
1952	122.2	. . .	107.7	14.5	. . .	. . .
1953	104.3	. . .	88.9	15.4	. . .	. . .
1954	125.6	. . .	81.6	. . .	. . .	44.0
1955	114.9	8.0	63.3	1.6	. . .	42.0
1956	115.5	. . .	59.5	14.0	. . .	42.0
1957	46.0	. . .	43.4	2.6	. . .	. . .
1958	119.7	37.8	41.9	. . .	. . .	40.0
1959	48.9	12.5	36.4	. . .	. . .	. . .
1960	118.6	109.1	9.5	. . .	. . .	. . .
1961	72.0	37.0	. . .	32.0	3.0	. . .
1962	49.5	45.9	3.6	. . .	. . .	. . .
1963	93.1	53.9	39.2	. . .	. . .	. . .
1964	117.4	104.2	13.2	. . .	. . .	. . .
1965	113.7	104.9	8.8	. . .	. . .	. . .
1966	149.9	68.9	8.4	(. . . . . 72.6[a] . . . .)		
Total 1952–66 of which	1,511.3[b]	582.2	605.4	80.1	3.0	168.0
Mexico and Panama	407.9[b]	362.9	. . .	. . .	. . .	. . .
Caribbean	184.9	88.3	96.6	. . .	. . .	. . .
South America	117.2[b]	41.0	9.9	38.1	3.0	. . .
Belgian Congo	225.0	15.0	. . .	42.0	. . .	168.0
Other Africa	468.3[b]	27.0	438.4	. . .	. . .	. . .
Asia	108.0	48.0	60.0	. . .	. . .	. . .

Sources: Based on data in United Nations, Department of Economics and Social Affairs, *World Economic Survey, 1965* (New York, 1966), Table 2–4, pp. 51–52; International Bank for Reconstruction and Development, *Annual Report, 1966–1967*, Table 11, p. 37.

[a] According to unpublished data compiled by the World Bank, these issues consist of a $6.0 million Peruvian corporate issue in Switzerland, a $2.4 million Government of Gabon issue in France, and $45.0 million Government of Mexico issues, $18.5 million Government of Peru issues, and a $0.7 Venezuelan corporate issue in unidentified markets and in currencies other than that of the market country.

[b] Includes issues described in the preceding footnote, not shown separately in the subtotals in the same row.

tal markets practically ceased their flotations of the less-developed countries' bonds from 1959 to 1965.[9] The waning of the European markets for the less-developed countries' bond issues coincided with the waxing of the New York market in the 1960's. From 1960 through 1965, bond

[9] Except for the Argentine issues of $32 million in Geneva and $3 million in Frankfurt, both in 1961.

issues of the less-developed countries in New York were considerably larger than those in all the other capital markets put together.

The strict compartmentalization of the European capital markets with regard to the less-developed countries' bond issues can also be seen from the data presented in Table 2.1. Throughout the period under discussion, all the less-developed countries' bond issues in London originated in the Sterling Area. Prior to 1966, Brussels catered to only the Belgian Congo's bonds before the latter's independence, Frankfurt had only a $3 million Argentine issue in 1961, and the $80 million bond issues of the less-developed countries sold in Geneva were all accounted for by the issues of three countries, Argentina, Peru, and the former Belgian Congo. In contrast, the borrowers in New York had a much wider geographic dispersion and were not limited to any particular currency areas, although even there, more than three-fourths of the less-developed countries' bond issues from 1952 to 1966 were floated by Mexico, Panama, and a few Caribbean countries. Where free access to a capital market is nominally open to all borrowers, as in Geneva and New York, such a high degree of compartmentalization calls for explanation and will be explored in Chapter 4.[10]

We turn now to a closer examination of the less-developed countries' new issues in the United States since the end of World War II. With greater availability of data on that market, we shall examine *all* new issues of the less-developed countries in that market, including both bond and corporate stock issues. In the case of corporate issues we shall include those of U.S. direct-investment companies abroad as well.[11]

---

[10] See pp. 62–67.

[11] For the purpose of balance-of-payments statistics, the U.S. Department of Commerce defines a "U.S. direct-investment company abroad" as one in which U.S. residents own at least a 25 percent equity interest and also exercise significant control of the management. See U.S. Department

TABLE 2.2. New Issues of the Less-developed Countries and Other Foreign Borrowers in the United States, 1946–65

(1)	(2) All Foreign	(3)	(4) IBRD &	(5)	(6) Other Developed	(7) Less- developed
Year	Borrowers	Canada	IADB[a]	Israel	Countries	Countries
	(millions of dollars)					
1946	182.2	142.7	...	...	31.4	8.1
1947	417.7	90.5	244.5	...	69.0	13.7
1948	150.0	150.0	...	...	...	...
1949	122.9	106.9	...	...	16.0	...
1950	320.3	230.3	80.0	...	...	10.1
1951	598.5	406.8	140.0	51.7	...	...
1952	327.9	171.1	110.0	46.8	...	...
1953	587.8	476.3	75.0	36.5	...	...
1954	432.1	266.7	100.0	40.0	25.0	0.4
1955	236.2	106.2	...	41.9	76.0	12.2
1956	669.0	567.7	...	53.0	47.0	1.3
1957	1,211.8	841.3	221.4	55.9	92.4	0.8
1958	1,354.7	526.3	419.8	47.0	320.7	40.9
1959	863.6	556.9	14.7	55.7	219.4	16.9
1960	688.2	285.8	108.6	50.9	115.0	127.9
1961	692.6	338.9	13.4	58.2	217.6	64.6
1962	1,343.8	550.6	180.5	60.2	503.8	48.6
1963	1,524.4	788.6	...	69.6	599.5	64.8
1964	1,226.9	792.1	154.5	107.4	56.0	115.0
1965	1,184.4	535.5	200.0	95.3	222.2	131.4
Total 1946–65	14,135.0	7,931.1	2,062.0	870.1	2,611.0	656.7

Sources: U.S. Department of Commerce, *The Balance of International Payments of the United States, 1946–1948,* 1950, pp. 264–65; *The Balance of Payments of the United States, 1949–1951,* 1952, p. 165; *New Foreign Securities Offered in the United States, 1952–1964,* Staff Working Paper in Economics and Statistics, No. 12 (July 1965). The 1965 data are supplied by the Balance of Payments Division of the U.S. Department of Commerce.
[a] International Bank for Reconstruction and Development and Inter-American Development Bank.

The data in Table 2.2 indicate that during the two decades 1946–65, foreigners issued slightly more than $14 billion in securities in the United States, of which Canadian borrowers alone accounted for more than one-half. Other developed countries (Col. 6) and the World Bank and the Inter-American Development Bank together (Col. 4) took up another one-third. All the less-developed coun-

of Commerce, *New Foreign Securities Offered in the United States, 1952–64,* Staff Working Paper in Economics and Statistics, No. 12 (July 1965), p. 2.

20   tries together (Col. 7) had only 5 percent, less than the total issues of Israel (Col. 5) alone in the same period.

During the first 12 years (1946–57) of the two decades, the U.S. foreign-securities market was predominated by the issues of Canada, the World Bank, and Israel, the three accounting for 92 percent of the total foreign issues in that period. The other developed countries and the less-developed countries began to increase their issues in substantial amounts in 1958. In the six years from 1958 through 1963, the "other developed countries" issued an annual average volume of $330 million, an increase of more than sevenfold compared to an average of only $40 million per year in the preceding six years. The less-developed countries issued an average volume of $60 million per year during the 1958–63 period, compared to an annual average of only $2.5 million during the preceding six years. The sharp decline in security issues of the "other developed countries" in the United States after 1963 reflected, of course, the effect of the U.S. Interest Equalization Tax on the purchase by U.S. residents of securities of such countries; whereas the issues of the less-developed countries, which are exempt from the Tax, continued to increase in 1964 and 1965, averaging $123 million in the two years—just about double the annual average issue during the preceding six years (1958–63).

Some historical perspective may be obtained by comparing the developments in the U.S. foreign-securities market during the two postwar decades 1946–65 with those during the 1920's. Annual data on the *public* issues of the less-developed countries and other foreign borrowers in the United States during the 1920's are presented in Table 2.3. Since the data for the prewar period do not cover issues privately placed with investing institutions, the resultant understatement of prewar issues in the data presented in Table 2.3 should be kept in mind when

TABLE 2.3. Public Issues of the Less-developed Countries and other Foreign Borrowers in the United States, 1920–29

Year	All Foreign Borrowers	Canada	Other Developed Countries	Less-developed Countries
	(millions of dollars)			
1920	585.9	189.4	347.5	49.0
1921	659.7	196.6	218.3	244.8
1922	813.7	226.8	230.0	356.9
1923	490.2	143.0	128.0	219.2
1924	1,209.2	277.4	736.4	195.4
1925	1,306.8	265.0	824.0	217.8
1926	1,270.2	308.8	536.2	425.2
1927	1,543.6	312.3	771.5	459.8
1928	1,482.1	237.4	805.3	439.4
1929	690.6	308.7	157.4	224.5
Total 1920–29	10,052.0	2,465.4	4,754.6	2,832.0

Source: Based on data in U.S. Department of Commerce, *Handbook of American Underwriting of Foreign Securities,* Trade Promotion Series, No. 104 (1930) Table 8, p. 19 and Appendix Table A, pp. 58–137.

they are compared with the postwar data in Table 2.2, which do include privately placed foreign issues.[12]

Even with this understatement, however, the data in Table 2.3 show that the foreign *public* issues in the United States averaged about $1 billion per year during the 1920's, considerably more than the average rate of total foreign issue of about $700 million a year during the two postwar decades of 1946–65. When account is taken of the approximate doubling of U.S. prices from the 1920's to the 1960's, the reduction in foreign issues in the United States is seen to be even sharper in real terms.

It is also interesting to observe the marked narrowing of the U.S. foreign-securities market in the postwar period as compared to the 1920's in terms of the geographic dis-

[12] Data on privately placed foreign issues in the United States for the 1920's are not available. It is known, however, that such issues increased rapidly in the postwar period, increasing from between 16 to 40 percent of total foreign issues in the 1952–60 period to about two thirds in the 1961–64 period. In 1963, for instance, private placements of foreign securities amounted to $1,089 million, compared to public issues of $436 million. See U.S. Department of Commerce, *New Foreign Securities,* p. 16, for 1963 data, and annual summary tables on pp. 12–54 for the other years.

persion of the borrowers in that market. Whereas Canada accounted for only one-fourth of the foreign issues in the market during the 1920's, its share became preponderant —56 percent—in the two postwar decades. The rest of the world, excluding the World Bank, the Inter-American Development Bank, and Israel, had 75 percent of the U.S. foreign-securities market in the 1920's, but had to share less than 25 percent of it in the two postwar decades. The less-developed countries as a group lost most ground: their share in the market fell from 28 percent during the 1920's to only 5 percent during the two postwar decades.

Annual data on the new issues of the less-developed countries in the United States from 1946 to 1965 are shown by countries of issue in Table 2.4. Table notations and footnotes provide information on whether and how much of the individual countries' issues were foreign-government issues, foreign-corporate issues, or issues of U.S. direct-investment companies in those countries.

As pointed out above, the first 12 years 1946–57 after the Second World War was a dormant period for the less-developed countries' borrowings in the U.S. securities market. The data in Table 2.4 show that throughout that period only six countries—Cuba, Panama, Argentina, Peru, Liberia, and the Philippines—made it to the market, and altogether the six issued only $46.5 million of securities, or less than 1 percent of the total foreign issues in the U.S. market. In five of the 12 years, not a single less-developed country was able to float any new issues in the market. Even more striking is the fact that aside from a $10 million refunding issue of the Republic of Panama in 1950 and an $8 million Republic of Cuba issue in 1955, all other issues from the less-developed countries during that period were floated by U.S. direct-investment companies in those countries.

The year 1958 appears to have been a turning point for the issues of both the less-developed and the developed

countries (other than Canada and Israel) in the United **23**
States. Upon closer examination, however, the upturn in
the less-developed countries' issues is seen to be largely
attributable to events directly or indirectly connected with
the World Bank's influence in that market. Out of a total
of $40.9 million of less-developed countries' issues in the
United States during that year, a $6 million Federation
of Rhodesia and Nyasaland issue was floated in June in a
joint operation with a $19 million World Bank loan to
that country; the $15 million Government of the Belgian
Congo issue in April had no overt link with World Bank
operations, but was offered only five months after a $40
million World Bank loan to that country and was managed
by a firm—Dillon, Read and Co. of New York—which had
been an active participant in most of the World Bank's
joint loan operations with private investors.[13] It seems to
be a safe presumption that neither issue could have been
successfully floated without some direct or indirect assistance from the World Bank. Inversely, it is suggested that
with direct or indirect assistance from the World Bank
other issues such as those two could be successfully floated
in the United States.

The year 1959 marked the emergence of a new group
of foreign borrowers in the U.S. market—the Caribbean
territories which are, or were until recently, British or
Dutch colonies. They have made resort to the market
every year since then.

The most dramatic turn of events, however, was the
rise of Mexico in 1960 as a major steady borrower in the
U.S. securities market. From 1960 through 1965, Mexico
issued $303 million in securities in the United States, ac-
counting for more than one-half of the total issues of the
less-developed countries in the United States during that
period. Its unique success in tapping the U.S. market

[13] See International Bank for Reconstruction and Development, *Thir-
teen Annual Report, 1957–1958*, pp. 12 and 24–25. The Belgian Congo
issue was not guaranteed by the Government of Belgium.

TABLE 2.4. New Issues of the Less-developed Countries in the United States, 1946-65 by Countries

	1946	1947	1950	1954	1955	1956	1957	Total 1946–57
			(millions of dollars)					
Cuba	0.35*	0.35*			12.2[a]			12.9
Panama	7.7	1.0*	10.0‡					18.7
Argentina		10.1*						10.1*
Peru		2.3*				1.3*		3.6*
Liberia							0.8*	0.8*
Philippines				0.4*				0.4*
Total	8.05*	13.75*	10.0‡	0.4*	12.2[a]	1.3*	0.8*	46.5

	1958	1959	1960	1961	1962	1963	1964	1965	Total 1958–65
Bahamas					11.0†				11.0†
Bermuda			16.0†	44.1†[b]					60.1†[b]
Jamaica		14.9[e]				1.5‡			16.4
Netherland Antilles					7.0†				7.0†
Trinidad						6.6†	7.5‡	10.0*	24.1
Mexico			80.6‡	17.7‡	20.0‡	43.1[d]	90.7[d]	51.4[d]	303.5
Panama	19.2[e]		31.3[e]		7.9†	9.3[e]			67.7
Colombia							2.5†		2.5†
Venezuela							6.3‡	15.5[f]	21.8
Malaysia								25.0‡	25.0‡

24

TABLE 2.4 (continued)

	1958	1959	1960	1961	1962	1963	1964	1965	Total 1958-65
Philippines	0.3*	...	...	...	...	0.5*	8.0*	23.5g	32.3
Belgian Congo	15.0‡	...	...	...	...	...	...	...	15.0‡
Gabon	...	...	...	...	...	3.8*	...	...	3.8*
Liberia	0.4*	2.0*	...	2.8*	2.7*	...	...	6.0†	13.9
Rhodesia and Nyasaland	6.0‡	...	...	...	...	...	...	...	6.0‡
Total	40.9	16.9	127.9	64.6	48.6	64.8	115.0	131.4	636.4

* Designates U.S. direct-investment issues.
† Foreign corporate issues.
‡ Foreign government issues.

a Cuba, 1955: an $8.0 million government issue and a $4.2 million U.S. direct-investment issue.
b Bermuda, 1961: including a corporate issue of unknown amount from the Netherland Antilles.
c Jamaica, 1959: $125 million in government issues and a $2.4 million U.S. direct-investment issue.
d Mexico, 1963: $40.0 million in government issues and a $3.1 million U.S. direct-investment issue. 1964: $60.0 million in government issues and $30.7 million in Mexican corporate issues. 1965: $35.4 million in government issues and $8 million each of direct-investment issues and of Mexican corporate issues.
e Panama, 1958: a $16.8 million government issue and a $2.4 million U.S. direct-investment issue. 1960: a $28.5 million Panamanian corporate issue and $2.8 million in U.S. direct-investment issues. 1963: a $9.3 million government issue and a $0.3 million Panamanian corporate issue.
f Venezuela, 1965: a $15.0 million government issue and a $0.5 million in Venezuelan corporate issues.
g Philippines, 1965: a $15.0 million government issue and $8.5 million in U.S. direct-investment issues.

should warrant our close attention in the chapters to follow.

Finally, it might be noted that there was a significant broadening of the U.S. securities market in 1965 for the issues of the less-developed countries. The governments of Malaysia, Philippines, and Venezuela all made their postwar debuts in the U.S. securities market in 1965. On the basis of unpublished data collected by the World Bank, this broadening process appears to have continued in 1966, though on a much reduced scale, when Algeria, Argentina, Bahamas, Jamaica, Mexico, Peru, and Venezuela issued $68.9 million in securities in the United States; but was drastically curtailed in the first three quarters of 1967, when only a $0.1 million Venezuelan corporate issue and a $11.3 million Government of Peru issue were reported in that market.[14]

[14] Four countries—Gabon, Mexico, Peru, and Venezuela—accounted for the $72.6 million of the less-developed countries' issues in 1966 in the Continental European and other (mainly Euro-dollar) markets. See footnote a, Table 2.1, p. 17. In the first three-quarters of 1967, Mexico alone issued a total of $95 million in Euro-dollar markets, but there were no other issues by the less-developed countries in international capital markets outside the United States.

CHAPTER THREE

POPULAR EXPLANATIONS FOR FAILURES TO FLOAT BONDS IN INTERNATIONAL MARKETS

WHY HAVE the less-developed countries on the whole had so little success during the postwar period in floating bonds in international capital markets? The answers to this question might differ widely, but these seem to be the explanations generally accepted by most observers: (1) the past debt defaults of the less-developed countries; (2) their political instability; (3) their existing debt burden; (4) the cost of borrowing; and (5) the legal and administrative hurdles for floating bonds in international markets.

This chapter makes an in-depth evaluation of each of these alleged factors in order to determine how significant they indeed have been in accounting for the failure of the less-developed countries to float large amounts of securities in international capital markets. Because of the greater availability of data on the U.S. new-issue market than on others, the analysis will be focused on the conditions and developments in the U.S. market in the 1946–65 period.

PAST DEBT DEFAULTS

A popular image is that U.S. investors have had painful experiences with foreign-bond defaults in the 1930's and 1940's, and hence are understandably wary of new foreign issues. Moreover, since bond defaults of the less-developed countries were far more extensive and lasted much longer than those of the developed countries, it appears obvious that investors in general should be much less receptive towards the less-developed countries' new issues than towards those of the developed countries. "Once burned, twice shy" seems to explain much of what has happened in the U.S. foreign-securities market in the last 20 some years.

A perusal of the history of foreign dollar-bond defaults during the 1930's and 1940's appears to substantiate this explanation. As the Great Depression swept over the world with a resultant collapse of the international monetary system, the less-developed countries were the first to default their foreign bonds in 1931.[15] By the end of 1935, when the first wave of defaults had subsided, a total of $2.9 billion in foreign dollar bonds were in default, amounting to 38.5 percent of the $7.5 billion publicly offered foreign dollar bonds then outstanding. Significantly, at that point most of the default countries were the less-developed countries, and the majority of the developed countries that had borrowed in the United States had either no default at all or only slight defaults on their dollar bonds.[16]

[15] Bolivia led the wave of foreign bond defaults by announcing on January 1, 1931, the suspension of service on all her foreign debts. Peru, Chile, Brazil, Colombia, Costa Rica, and Panama all followed suit in the same year.

[16] For the purpose of this statement, the Eastern European countries now in the Soviet bloc are included among the "less-developed countries." At the end of 1935, the only developed countries that were in complete

World War II brought forth a second wave of foreign-
bond defaults which swept most of the developed countries under as well.[17] After the end of the war, however,
all the developed countries, except such wartorn countries
as Austria, Germany, Italy, and Japan,[18] resumed payments on their dollar issues, and had by the end of 1950
either completely paid off all such debts or were servicing
them according to the original terms of the bonds. The
postwar debt-service performance of the less-developed
countries varied widely. By the end of 1950, some of them
had retired all their dollar debts; others were servicing in
full; many made unilateral adjustment offers and were
servicing on an adjusted basis; a few remained in complete
default.[19] Subsequently, the few countries remaining in
default at the end of 1950 one by one reached debt-settlement agreements with their foreign bondholders.[20] By the
end of 1962, all the countries except the Republic of
the Congo,[21] outside of the Sino-Soviet bloc, had settled

default with respect to their dollar bonds were Germany, Greece, and
Sweden; Canada and Denmark had only slight defaults, 3.1 and 0.7 per-
cent respectively of their outstanding dollar bonds. In contrast, all the
less-developed countries, except Haiti, had either completely defaulted
their dollar bonds or had substantial portions of such bonds in default:
Argentina, 25.3 percent; Cuba, 60.5 percent; and Panama, 77.6 percent.
Data are derived from John T. Madden, Marcus Nadler, and Harry C.
Sauvain, *America's Experience as a Creditor Nation* (New York: Prentice-
Hall, 1937), Appendix II, pp. 308–9.

[17] At the end of 1944, the only countries still maintaining full service
on all their dollar bonds were Australia, Finland, France, Guatemala, Ire-
land, and Liberia; in addition, Argentina had only 0.5 percent, Uruguay
3.6 percent, Canada 5.3 percent, and Panama 8.9 percent of their outstanding dollar bonds in default. See Foreign Bondholders Protective Council,
Report, 1941–1944 (New York, 1945), pp. 806–7.

[18] Also excepted are Greece, which did not reach an agreement with
her U.S. bondholders until 1962, and all the Eastern European countries
in the Soviet bloc, whose dollar bonds are still in complete default. Yugoslavia is the only communist country that has made a debt-adjustment
offer found to be acceptable by the (U.S.) Foreign Bondholders Protective
Council—in August 1964.

[19] See Foreign Bondholders Protective Council, *Report, 1950* (New
York, 1951), pp. 212–13, and also Hans J. Dernburg, "Foreign Dollar Bonds:
Present Status and Possibilities of Future Financing," *The Journal of
Finance*, V, No. 3 (September 1950), 217–40.

[20] Costa Rica in 1952, Ecuador in 1953, and Bolivia in 1957.

[21] For the case of the Congo, see the discussion on p. 34.

their dollar-bond debts and resumed payments either in full or on an adjusted basis.

This brief review of the foreign-bond defaults and default settlements indicates that as a group the less-developed countries indeed have had poorer debt-servicing records than the developed countries outside the Sino-Soviet bloc. Many investors must have suffered substantial losses in the less-developed countries' foreign bonds. Even in those cases where the debtor country had nominally retired all its foreign bonds, such bonds were often purchased from the market at a fraction of their original cost to the investors. Where servicing was resumed on an adjusted basis, bondholders in most cases have had to accept greatly reduced payments in comparison to the original terms of the bonds. The bad taste of loss lingers long, so it is claimed, and makes investors suspicious of foreign bonds in general and the less-developed countries' bonds in particular.

The importance of this factor, however, can easily be exaggerated. First of all, although the general impression is that investors have suffered heavy losses in foreign bonds and especially in the less-developed countries' bonds, the extent of their losses through the last 30 some years has not been ascertained. The only serious effort at a statistical measurement, to my knowledge, was made by John T. Madden and his associates,[22] using data to the end of 1935. But by then, most of the less-developed countries' foreign-bond defaults had already taken place and the investors' losses on these bonds had already been incurred at least on paper. The study attempted to measure the "net total gain or loss" of U.S. investors on their investments in the non-Canadian foreign bonds issued in the 1920–31 period. It compares, on one hand, the total amount of purchases

[22] Madden *et al.*, *America's Experience as a Creditor Nation*, pp. 138–52.

of such issues by U.S. residents with, on the other hand, the sum of the interest and amortization payments arising from these bonds received by them up to the end of 1935 plus the total market value of these bonds outstanding on that date. If the former was larger than the latter, the U.S. investors as a whole were supposed to have sustained a net total loss on their investments in such bonds; if the former was smaller than the latter, they were assumed to have had a net total gain. On the basis of such calculations, the authors concluded that U.S. investments in non-Canadian foreign bonds issued in the 1920–31 period resulted in a net total gain of about $1.8 billion at the end of 1935. Although much of the gain was attributable to the net profits made on the bonds of the developed countries, the losses from the less-developed countries' bonds of that period were not nearly as large as they were commonly presumed to be. For instance, U.S. investors as a whole had a net total loss of only $58.5 million from their investments in Latin American bonds of that period, compared to a total of $1.9 billion in such bonds outstanding at the end of 1935.

In short, the evidences gathered in the study by Madden and his associates cast doubt on the popular impression that U.S. investors as a whole suffered serious losses on their investments during the 1920's in foreign bonds in general, and in bonds of the less-developed countries in particular. What statistical data that are available simply do not bear out that impression.

Secondly, if experiences in other international securities markets are any guide, investors are not long deterred by past defaults from making new investments in foreign bonds. The defaults of the 1930's and the 1940's were American investors' first experience with the vicissitudes of foreign-bond investments. However, as Madden, Nadler, and Sauvain point out:

The history of foreign lending is replete with defaults. During the nineteenth century every major downward swing of the business cycle caused the failure of governments and other foreign borrowers to meet their external obligations. . . . It is significant that these periods of foreign bond defaults did not permanently deter the British from making foreign investments. In most cases the suspension of interest payments were temporary and, with improvement in world economic conditions, the defaults were adjusted, often with little or no ultimate loss to investors.[23]

There is no ground to presume that U.S. investors today are characteristically different from British investors in the nineteenth century, and that, "with improvement in world economic conditions," they would not resume investing in the less-developed countries' bonds as British investors did in the nineteenth century. In other words, by itself, past debt-default records should not be a serious deterrent to a country's new issues in the market.

Thirdly, this hypothesis seems to be borne out by Mexico's experience in the U.S. new-issue market in the 1960's. As shown in Table 2.4 (p. 24), during the postwar years Mexico has been the most successful borrower among the less-developed countries in the U.S. securities market. Yet its debt record prior to its reentry into the market in 1960 was anything but immaculate. Mexico was a major borrower in international capital markets during the nineteenth century. Its debt record, however, was marred almost from the start of its foreign borrowings by defaults dating back to as early as 1827.[24] After the Revolution of 1910, the entire Mexican external debt went into default in 1914. Throughout the interwar period, negotiations for debt settlement were tortuous and debt payments intermittent. The government of Mexico made final offers of debt settlement in 1942 and in 1946 on different portions of Mexico's external debts, and began payments

[23] Madden *et al.*, *America's Experience as a Creditor Nation,* pp. 107–8.
[24] See International Bank for Reconstruction and Development, *The Economic Development of Mexico,* Report of the Combined Mexican Working Party (Baltimore: Johns Hopkins Press, 1953), p. 139.

to bondholders who acceded to such offers. The offers, however, have never been accepted by the Foreign Bond-holders Protective Council and were denounced by the Council as involving "a reduction of principal, cancellation of a very large part of the back interest, payment of the current interest at an exceedingly low rate, and discrimination in favor of certain issues of 'secured bonds.' "[25] In July 1960, the Mexican government paid off all its pre-1914 external debts under the terms of its 1942 and 1946 offers.[26] All this is, of course, not to cast doubt on the creditworthiness of Mexican bonds, but rather to show that perhaps past debt record is in fact not as important a factor in investors' minds as is often presumed.

Lastly, even if debt record is an important consideration, there is no reason to believe that the records of the 1930's and 1940's are necessarily more pertinent than those of more recent years. Since the end of the war, the less-developed countries have incurred and have been servicing huge amounts of external debts to foreign governments, international agencies, foreign banks, and commercial suppliers. Aside from defaults attributable to political upheavals to be considered in the next section, there have been very few defaults compared to the total magnitudes of these debts outstanding.

POLITICAL INSTABILITY

Rightly or wrongly, the less-developed countries are often associated in the popular mind with revolutions, coup d'etats, civil wars, and, hence, with poor debt risks. Events in recent years especially seem to lend support to this view. Thus, Cuba, having maintained a relatively respectable debt record through the Depression and War

[25] See the Council's *Report, 1962–1964* (New York, 1965), pp. 103–4.
[26] Except for $45 million in dollar bonds and £3 million sterling in bonds unilaterally nullified by the Mexican government. See *prospectus* of the United Mexican States External Bonds of 1963, offered by Kuhn, Loeb and Co. and the First Boston Corp. on July 16, 1963, p. 50.

34   years, defaulted on all its dollar bonds—a total of $52.4
million outstanding—on December 31, 1960, two years
after the establishment of the Castro regime. The Republic of the Congo in 1961, amid civil war and general
collapse of the government apparatus, defaulted on its
external debts, of which $15 million was in dollar bonds
issued in the United States in 1958.[27] It so happens that
the only two major foreign-bond defaults in the postwar
period are both attributable to political upheavals in the
borrowing countries.

However, to generalize from these two instances as
reflecting the creditworthiness of the less-developed countries' bond issues is clearly unwarranted. Although the
political situation is still very much in a state of flux in a
number of less-developed countries, it is not the case in
the majority of the less-developed countries. Moreover,
even where the political future is not so clear, there should
be no presumption equating political uncertainty with
poor financial risks. In Latin America, for instance, a
fairly well-established tradition has directed that one of
a new government's first acts after coming into power by
revolution or coup d'etat, is a proclamation to assure the
continued observance of all the country's external obligations lest diplomatic recognition and the nation's international credit standing be endangered.[28] In this age of close

[27] The portion purchased by U.S. residents, however, amounted to
only $3.35 million. See U.S. Department of Commerce, *New Foreign
Securities Offered in the United States, 1952–64,* Staff Working Paper in
Economics and Statistics, No. 12 (July 1965), p. 39.
Although the bond was not guaranteed by Belgium, it was covered by
the treaty signed by the Congo and Belgium on February 6, 1965, providing
for settlement of public debts of the former Belgian Congo. According to
the terms of the treaty, a Belgian-Congolese Redemption and Management
Fund was set up, with capital provided by both governments, to handle
the settlement. On April 20, 1966, the fund published an order to exchange the 1958 dollar bonds for an equivalent amount of Belgian-franc
bonds redeemable in 40 years. For detail, see *Moody's Municipal and
Government Manual: American and Foreign, February 1967* (New York:
Moody's, 1967), p. 2960.
[28] See Madden *et al., America's Experience as a Creditor Nation,* p.
212, which cites a case during a period of political disturbance in the early

international economic interdependence, the smooth functioning of a nation's foreign trade and economic development programs is so vitally dependent on the continued lubrication of foreign banking and trade credits that a foreign-bond default, which could trigger a major confidence crisis, would be unthinkable except in the direst circumstances.

That this view is not mere fantasy or wishful thinking is evidenced by the fact that long-term bilateral *private* capital flows from the developed market-economy countries to the less-developed countries during the period from 1960 to 1965 amounted to more than $17 billion.[29] If other types of private investments—not all of which were protected by the various national and international investment-guaranty or protective schemes[30]—have so far not been visibly deterred by the alleged political instability in the less-developed countries, it would seem hard to justify that as a major deterrent to investment in the bond issues of the less-developed countries in international capital markets.

This is not to say that political instability in the less-developed countries is, or should be, of no consideration to investors in these countries' bond issues. It would probably be a major consideration with respect to prospective issues of a number of the less-developed countries, but would not likely be so in the majority of cases. Nevertheless, these risks are undeniably there, and any measures

---

history of Chile, when both of the rival governments transferred funds to foreign bankers to meet external debt service.

[29] See Organization for Economic Cooperation and Development, *Development Assistance Efforts and Policies, 1966 Review* (Paris, 1966), Table II, p. 30.

[30] For U.S. Government schemes, *see* Marina Von Neumann Whitman, *Government Risk-Sharing in Foreign Investment* (Princeton: Princeton University Press, 1966). For national schemes to provide export-credit insurance, see United Nations, Department of Economic and Social Affairs, *Export Credits and Development Financing* (New York, 1967), two volumes, especially Part 2. For international schemes to settle investment disputes and provide investment insurance, see IBRD, *Annual Report, 1966–1967* (Washington, 1967), pp. 6–17 and 20.

36   that could help reduce these risks would also tend to assist the flotation of the less-developed countries' bond issues in international capital markets. That is a point we need to keep in mind (as we get to Chapter 6) in suggesting a scheme for the attainment of that objective.

EXISTING DEBT BURDEN

Much concern has been expressed in recent years over the mounting debt burdens of the less-developed countries.[31] In 1964 the external debt of these countries amounted to about $40 billion—much larger than their total export earnings that year—and total interest and amortization payments were about $5 billion, well over one-half of the net flow to these countries of long-term capital and donations from the developed countries.[32] Approximately three-fourths of this debt was owed or guaranteed by the governments of these countries. From 1962 to 1965, such public and publicly guaranteed debts grew at an annual rate of 16 percent from $25 billion at the end of 1962 to $39 billion at the end of 1965. Service payments on these debts increased during the same period at an annual rate of 10 percent, considerably faster than the growth rate of the less-developed countries' total exports of goods and services.[33]

The external-debt situation varies considerably from country to country. During the 1962–65 period, the average ratio of annual debt-service payments to annual ex-

[31] See in particular, Dragoslav Avramovic, *Debt Servicing Capacity and Postwar Growth in International Indebtedness* (Baltimore: Johns Hopkins Press, 1958); Dragoslav Avramovic and Ravi Gulhati, *Debt Servicing Problems of Low-Income Countries* (Baltimore: Johns Hopkins Press, 1960); Dragoslav Avramovic *et al., Economic Growth and External Debt* (Baltimore: Johns Hopkins Press, 1964); Organization for Economic Cooperation and Development, *Development Assistance Efforts and Policies* (Paris), recent annual reviews; International Bank for Reconstruction and Development, recent *Annual Reports;* United Nations, Department of Economic and Social Affairs, *World Economic Survey, 1965* (New York, 1966), pp. 89–99.
[32] See U.N., *World Economic Survey, 1965,* p. 89.
[33] See IBRD, *Annual Report, 1966–1967,* p. 30.

ports of goods and services ranged from about 28 percent for Argentina and Brazil, and nearly 20 percent for Chile and Mexico, to less than 2 percent for Jamaica, Ceylon, Malaysia, and Singapore.[34] The growth rates of public and publicly guaranteed debt also varied widely, ranging from over 30 percent a year for Sudan, India, and Pakistan to less than 10 percent a year for Brazil, Malaysia, Uruguay, and Venezuela, during the 1956–64 period.[35] Also notable are the wide differences among the maturity structures of the less-developed countries' external debts: The proportion of external debt outstanding at the end of 1962 repayable during 1963–67 was estimated to be more than half for Venezuela, Mexico, Guatemala, Israel, the Philippines, and Iran, but less than one-fifth for Rhodesia and Nyasaland, Malaysia, and East Africa (Kenya, Tanzania, Uganda, and the Common Services Organization combined).[36]

Excessive debt accumulation coupled with awkward bunching of debt maturities could precipitate payments crises during times of abrupt shortfall in export earnings, as occurred in the 1930's. Outright debt defaults have been avoided since 1945—except those of the Congo and Cuba attributable to political disturbances—largely through debt re-scheduling operations negotiated with the creditors, such as the debt re-settlements of Argentina in 1956, 1963, and 1965; Brazil in 1961 and 1964; Chile in 1964; Uruguay in 1965 and 1966; Ghana and Indonesia in 1966.[37] Such operations inevitably cast doubt on the capacity of future borrowings by these countries and perhaps also had adverse effects on the bond flotations of other less-developed countries.

In view of these developments, how likely is it that

[34] *Ibid.*, pp. 32–33.
[35] See U.N., *World Economic Survey, 1965*, Figure XII, p. 91.
[36] See U.N., *World Economic Survey, 1965*, Figure XIV, p. 92.
[37] See U.N., *World Economic Survey, 1965*, p. 93, and Organization for Economic Cooperation and Development, *Development Assistance Efforts and Policies, 1966 Review* (Paris, 1966), p. 115.

investors would respond favorably to new issues of the less-developed countries in international capital markets? Moreover, even if the investors could be induced to do so, would a substantial expansion of the less-developed countries' new issues be in the long-run interests of both the lenders and the borrowers alike?

On the first question, generalizations are not likely to be helpful. As pointed out above, the external-debt situation varies widely from country to country. Each case will have to be examined individually. It may, nevertheless, be pertinent to observe that heavy debt accumulation has not been a serious detriment to Mexico's foreign borrowings through bond issues. Perhaps, by most criteria, Mexico already has had a "debt burden" much heavier than most of the less-developed countries;[38] yet it has been one of the most successful borrowers in international bond markets in recent years.

As to the desirability of increasing the bond issues of less-developed countries that are already heavily laden with external debt, it should be kept in mind that a substantial expansion in a country's foreign issues need not imply a large increase in its total external debt. A major element in the debt burden of many less-developed countries is the high proportion of short and medium-term suppliers' credits in their external debts. For instance, the share of payments on such credits in total debt-service payments in 1965 was estimated to be 63 percent for Brazil, 59 percent for Argentina, and 60 percent for Nigeria.[39] Bond issues for the replacement of short and medium-term

[38] According to data on a number of "indicators of debt-servicing capacity" selected by the U.N. Department of Economic and Social Affairs, Mexico's average ratio of debt service to export earnings in the 1962–64 period was 20.1 percent, among the highest for the 28 less-developed countries being compared; its debt-service payment increased at an average annual rate of 22 percent from 1956 to 1964, compared to a growth rate of export receipts of only 3 percent and of official reserves of only 1.6 percent during the same period. See U.N., *World Economic Survey, 1965*, Annex Table A.III.1, p. 99.

[39] See IBRD, *Annual Report, 1966–1967*, p. 32.

suppliers' credits could make a significant contribution to the improvement of these countries' debt-maturity structures and thereby towards a lessening of their debt burdens, without increasing the total sizes of their external debt. Moreover, insofar as the cost of borrowing through bond issues is lower than that through suppliers' credit,[40] the substitution should also soften the average terms of capital flow to these countries.

To suggest substitution of bond issues for suppliers' credits as a source of finance does not mean that bond issues should be limited to that purpose. Whether or not they should be so limited, of course, depends on whether or not the debt burden of the country in question is already "too large." The crux of the matter, then, falls on the question: When is a country's external-debt burden too large?

Unfortunately, the concept of "debt burden" of a country is not easily quantifiable. The rule of thumb commonly used is the so-called "debt-service ratio," expressing the country's annual interest and amortization payments on external debt as a ratio of its annual earnings from exports of goods and services. It is useful as an indicator of the proportion of the country's current foreign-exchange earnings pre-empted by debt-service payments. However, its limitations are many.[41] A cash-flow concept, it includes amortization payments as a charge against current export earnings—a rather unusual practice, since debt, whether of a corporation or of a country, is normally rolled over and not expected to be repaid out of a year's income. Moreover, as a purely static concept, its usefulness in measuring a country's long-run capacity for external-debt service in the context of growth is virtually nil. The relevant consideration should be how easily the borrower will be able to service its debts in the future, not how hard

[40] See discussion in next section, pp. 44–45.
[41] For a penetrating analysis, see Avramovic *et al.*, *Economic Growth and External Debt*, pp. 13–43.

it has been to service its old debts out of its current earnings.

An adequate evaluation of a country's long-run capacity of debt-service must take into account the country's long-run growth potential, the prospective developments in its balance of payments, the size of its foreign reserves, the availability of external compensatory finance for coping with payments contingencies, the compressibility of its imports, and so on. It is gratifying to note in this connection that a promising start in the formulation of such a theory has been made by the staff of the World Bank. Preliminary results of its studies suggest that, given "reasonable" assumptions of a debtor-country's output growth rate, domestic savings rate, capital-output ratio, export growth rate, and so on, it could sustain a rapidly increasing debt-service-export earnings ratio that reaches a peak as high as more than 50 percent, before gradually decreasing until it reaches zero at the end of a 36-year debt cycle.[42] Although at present, the theory is important more for its potential development than for its immediate applicability to particular situations, it would seem to suggest that the present anxiety over "high" debt-service ratios of a number of the less-developed countries may not be at all warranted.[43]

COST OF BORROWING AND RETURN TO INVESTOR

The high cost of borrowing through bond issues has at times been mentioned as a possible deterrent to the less-

---

[42] See Avramovic *et al., Economic Growth and External Debt,* pp. 47–84, and Essay IV with Mathematical Appendix, pp. 154–92. An earlier version of the model was given in Gerald M. Alter, "The Servicing of Foreign Capital Inflows by Underdeveloped Countries," in *Economic Development for Latin America,* edited by Howard S. Ellis (London: Macmillan, 1962), pp. 139–60; see also comments and discussion on the paper in pp. 160–67.

[43] David Finch's 1951 study shows that, during the early 1930's, Canada's and Australia's debt-service ratios reached as high as 37 and 44 percent respectively while maintaining nearly perfect debt-service records, and then fell away to only 8 percent in both cases in the late 1940's. See David Finch, "Investment Service of Underdeveloped Countries," *International*

developed countries' bond flotations in international capi- tal markets. Since this assertion relates to *ex ante* motivations, it is nearly impossible to find direct evidence either to substantiate or to refute it on the basis of actual flotation costs. Even though such a *direct* substantiation or refutation of the proposition is not attempted here, it may nevertheless be of interest to see how high such costs have actually been and to compare them with the costs of borrowing from other sources. Moreover, insofar as the yield of a bond to the investor differs from its cost to the borrower,[44] it should also be pertinent to compare the yields of the less-developed countries' bond issues with those obtainable from alternative avenues of investment, as a measure of the extra incentives that have been necessary to attract investors to the less-developed countries' bonds.

Table 3.1 presents data on the borrowing costs and yields to maturity of ten public issues of the less-developed countries' bonds in the United States from 1958 through 1965. The ten issues were all direct obligations of the national governments of the respective countries and include most of the public issues of these countries in the United States during those eight years.

The ensuing analysis based on data presented in Table 3.1 may be divided into three parts: (1) non-interest costs of bond flotation, (2) effective interest cost, and (3) return to investors.

(1) *Non-interest costs of bond flotation.* The non-interest costs consist of the underwriting spread between

---

Monetary Fund Staff Papers, II, No. 1 (September 1951), Tables 4 and 5, 77–80. Finch's data include direct-investment earnings and exclude amortization payments, hence are not directly comparable with the debt-service ratios for the less-developed countries cited on p. 37.

[44] In the case of a public issue, the cost to the borrower exceeds the return to the investor by the amount of discounts and commissions paid to security underwriters plus a lump sum for the reimbursement of such flotation expenses as publicity, printing of bonds, stamp duty and registration fees. Most of these expenses can be avoided in direct placements with investors, although the total cost of borrowing—interest plus flotation cost—may not be any lower.

TABLE 3.1. Borrowing Costs and Maturity Yields of Ten Public Issues of the Less-developed Countries in the United States, 1958–65

(1) Issuing Country	(2) Date	(3) Amount	(4) Term	(5) Coupon Rate	(6) Price to Investor	(7) Yield to Investor	(8) Under-writing Spread	(9) Proceeds to Issuer	(10) Effective Interest Cost	(11) Expense Reimburse-ment
	(mo./yr.)	(millions of dollars)	(years)	(%)						(thousands of dollars)
Belgian Congo	4/58	15.0	15	5.25	98.50	5.40	2.75	95.75	5.67	50
Rhodesia and Nyasaland	6/58	6.0	15	5.75	97.50	6.00	3.50	94.00	6.38	40
Panama	11/58	16.8	35	4.80	101.17	4.73	1.00	100.17	4.79	n.a.[a]
Jamaica	2/59	10.0	15	5.75	95.50	6.22	2.75	92.75	6.51	32.5
Mexico	7/63	25.0	15	6.75	97.70	7.00	3.75	93.95	7.42	125
Mexico	4/64	25.0	15	6.50	97.66	6.75	3.50	94.16	7.13	100
Mexico	10/64	35.0	15	6.25	98.25	6.43	3.375	97.875	6.80	75
Philippines	1/65	15.0	25	6.50	98.50	6.66	3.50	95.00	6.92	n.a.[a]
Venezuela	4/65	15.0	25	6.25	99.00	6.33	3.375	95.625	6.62	n.a.[a]
Mexico	10/65	27.5	15	6.50	98.75	6.63	3.25	95.50	6.99	60

Sources: *Moody's Municipal and Government Manual: American and Foreign, February 1967* (New York: Moody's; and a facsimile of worksheets (dated November 21, 1963) compiled by and supplied to the author through the courtesy of Kuhn, Loeb and Co., New York.

[a] Data not available.

the price of a bond to the investors and its gross proceeds
to the issuer, and the reimbursement of expenses to the
bond underwriters.

It is notable from the data in Table 3.1 that the underwriting spreads of the less-developed countries' bonds,
with the exception of three issues,[45] were all well above
3 percent of the face value of the bonds. They compare
with the standard 2.5 percent paid by almost all the national governments, and between 2.7 percent and 3 percent by the government agencies and local governments
of the developed countries during the postwar years.[46] As
to the reimbursement of expenses to underwriters, the
available data do not permit any meaningful generaliza-
tion. On one hand, the amounts paid by Belgian Congo,
the Federation of Rhodesia and Nyasaland, and Jamaica
were all within the range of between 25 and 50 thousand
dollars paid by most national governments of the less-
developed countries in their public issues in the United
States. On the other hand, the reimbursement on the
first postwar Government of Mexico issues in the United
States in 1963 amounted to $125,000, then gradually ta-
pered down to $60,000 on its issues in 1965. To what ex-
tent Mexico's experience is typical of those of other less-
developed countries cannot be determined from the data
now available.[47]

[45] The three exceptions are the Belgian Congo, Panama, and Jamaica
issues.

[46] Based on data supplied through the courtesy of Kuhn, Loeb and Co.
of New York. See Table 3.1.

[47] The non-interest costs of foreign-bond flotation have been found to
be much lower in New York than in other international financial centers.
A Bank of England compilation found in 1963 that such costs for foreign
governments ranged between 1.25 and 4.75 percent in the United States,
but between 4.25 and 4.5 percent in the United Kingdom, 3.5 and 5 percent in Switzerland, and 4 and 5 percent in the Netherlands. See Bank of
England, *Quarterly Bulletin*, III, No. 2 (June 1963), 106–17. Another set
of data compares the initial flotation costs plus the recurrent non-interest
costs—e.g., withholding tax on interest payments and commission paid to
the fiscal agent for handling such payments—for industrial loans in various
international financial centers: about 1.5 percent of the nominal amount
of the issue in the United States, 2.8 percent in the United Kingdom, 3.2
percent in Switzerland, and 3.5 percent in the Netherlands. See *The Times*
(London), April 16, 1963, p. 16.

(2) *Effective interest costs.* The effective interest cost to the issuer is calculated on the basis of the coupon rate, the terms to maturity, and the actual gross proceeds to the issuer before deduction of reimbursement of expenses to the underwriters. Except for the 1958 Government of Panama issue,[48] the effective interest costs of the less-developed countries' issues in the United States were, as to be expected, considerably higher than those of the developed countries. Two examples should suffice to illustrate this: The Belgian Congo issue in April 1958 cost 5.67 percent as compared to 5.09 percent for the Commonwealth of Australia bonds issued in the same month; the Government of Jamaica paid 6.51 percent for its February 1959 issue, compared to the 6.03 percent of the Kingdom of Denmark issue in the same month.[49]

As might be expected, the interest costs of bond issues in the United States have been found to be significantly lower than those in most of the other international financial centers.[50] But, in view of the strict compartmentalization of European issue markets noted (p. 18), the relevant comparison seems not to be between the costs of bond issues in different capital markets, but between the costs of bond issues on one hand and those of borrowings from alternative sources on the other. For the latter comparison, we turn to the data on the weighted average terms of newly incurred external public debt of 34 less-developed countries by various sources in 1964, compiled and published by the World Bank, and summarized in Table 3.2.

The data in Table 3.2 indicate that, whereas the average rate of interest cost of 5.48 percent on the less-devel-

[48] The cost of the Panamanian issue was exceptionally low, presumably because it was an issue secured by first charge and lien on U.S. government annual treaty payments to Panama.

[49] Data supplied through the courtesy of Kuhn, Loeb and Co. of New York. See Table 3.1.

[50] For a comparison of such costs in different international capital markets for the years 1954, 1958, and 1963, see U.N. *World Economic Survey, 1965* (New York, 1966), Table II-7, p. 56.

TABLE 3.2. Weighted Average Terms of External Public Debt of 34 Less-developed Countries by Various Sources, 1964

	Contractual Amount	Rate of Interest	Grace Period	Terms of Maturity
	(millions of dollars)	%	*(years)*	*(years)*
Publicly issued bonds	96	5.48	3.0	15.0
Privately placed debts[a]	1,039	6.01	1.2	5.8
Multilateral loans	1,015	3.65	6.7	33.7
Total bilateral loans[b]	1,861	3.50	6.6	26.9
Loans from Sino-Soviet countries	15	3.09	1.5	5.0
Total external public debt	4,025	4.23	5.1	22.8

Source: International Bank for Reconstruction and Development, *Annual Report, 1965–1966* (Washington, 1966), p. 37, Table 10.
[a] Includes suppliers' credits, settlement for nationalized properties, and credits from various sources.
[b] Excluding Sino-Soviet countries.

oped countries' publicly issued external bonds was much higher than the average rates of between 3.09 and 3.65 percent on loans from multilateral institutions and individual developed countries, it was nevertheless significantly lower than the average of 6.01 percent they paid on privately placed debts—mainly suppliers' credits—in 1964. Similar observations may be made with regard to the length of the grace period, i.e., the duration before interest and principal payments begin, and the terms to maturity of the various types of loans. On the whole, the impression gained from these comparisons is unmistakable: in 1964 the 34 less-developed countries contracted more than $1 billion of privately placed debts at terms far more costly and stringent than those for the mere $96 million of bonds they publicly offered in international capital markets. If so, then obviously the cost of borrowing could not have been as serious a deterrent to the less-developed countries' bond issues in international markets as is sometimes presumed.

(3) *Return to investors.* We turn now to a comparison of the yields to investors of the less-developed countries' issues in the United States with those of other types

TABLE 3.3. Yields to Investors of Less-developed Countries' Issues in the United States Compared to Yields of High-grade U.S. Domestic Corporate Bonds and of Canadian Issues in the United States, 1958–65

(1) Issuing Country[a]	(2) Date of Issue	(3) Yield to Investor	(4) Corporate Bond Yield[b]	(5) Premium Over Corp. Bond Yield	(6) Canadian Bond Yield[c]	(7) Premium Over Can. Bond Yield
	(mo./yr.)	(%)	(%)	(%)	(%)	(%)
Belgian Congo	4/58	5.40	3.60	50	4.12	31
Rhodesia & Nyasaland	6/58	6.00	3.57	68	4.15	45
Jamaica	2/59	6.22	4.14	50	4.75	31
Mexico[d]	2/61	6.875	4.27	61	5.25	31
Mexico[d]	6/62	7.00	4.28	64	5.25	33
Bahamas[d][e]	10/62	6.27	4.28	46	5.25	19
Jamaica[d]	2/63	7.00	4.19	67	4.94	42
Mexico	7/63	7.00	4.26	64	4.75	47
Mexico	4/64	6.75	4.40	53	5.00	35
Venezuela[d][e]	8/64	5.25	4.41	19	4.75	11
Mexico	10/64	6.43	4.42	45	4.75	35
Philippines	1/65	6.66	4.43	50	4.76	40
Venezuela	4/65	6.35	4.43	43	4.75	34
Mexico	10/65	6.63	4.56	45	4.875	36

Sources: Col. (1)–(3) and (6): U.S. Department of Commerce, *New Foreign Securities Offered in the United States, 1952–64,* Staff Working Paper in Economics and Statistics, No. 12 (July 1965); and data supplied by the Department of Commerce. Col. (4) *Supplement to Banking & Monetary Statistics, Section 12: Money Rates and Securities Markets,* Board of Governors of the Federal Reserve System (Washington D.C., 1966), pp. 68–73; and *Federal Reserve Bulletin,* various issues. Col. (5) = (3)/(4) — 1. Col. (7) = (3)/(6) — 1.
  [a] Publicly issued government bonds, except otherwise noted.
  [b] Monthly average of daily figures in Moody's series for corporate bonds with Aaa rating.
  [c] Yields on selected Canadian provincial or municipal bonds issued in the United States.
  [d] Privately placed.
  [e] Corporate bonds.

of bonds in that market. In Table 3.3 are presented data on the maturity yields of 14 less-developed countries' issues floated in the years 1958–65, to be compared with the average yields on high grade U.S. domestic corporate bonds during the same months in which the less-developed countries' bonds were issued, and the maturity yields on Canadian provincial or municipal issues in the United States floated in the same months as the less-developed countries' issues.[51] The domestic-bond yield is used as a barometer of the capital-market condition in the United States. The selection of a Canadian-bond yield as a benchmark for comparison is based on the consideration that perhaps those who buy foreign bonds are investors of a special genre, viz. those who are willing to take greater risks for the sake of higher returns,[52] and hence Canadian issues may be a closer substitute to the less-developed countries' issues than U.S. domestic bonds.

The percentage premiums of the yields on the less-developed countries' issues over the U.S. domestic-bond yields and the yields on Canadian issues are presented in columns (5) and (7) of Table 3.3. With the exception of two privately placed corporate issues, all the other issues of the less-developed countries listed in the table provided their investors a return between nearly one-half and two-thirds higher than that of high grade U.S. domestic corporate bonds, and between one-third and nearly one-half higher than that on Canadian issues. These premiums in the postwar years were significantly greater than those which prevailed in the 1920's. According to U.S. Department of Commerce data, Latin American public issues in the United States from 1919 to 1929 yielded, on a weighted average, 6.97 percent—about 41 percent higher than the average yield on high grade U.S. domestic corporate bonds and 25 percent higher than the average yield on Canadian public issues in the United States during the same years.[53]

The higher premiums on the less-developed countries' issues in recent years than those prevailing in the 1920's provide a measure of the investors' greater wariness toward less-developed countries' securities than in the

[51] In a few cases, the following month.
[52] For a similar view, see Ilse Mintz, *Deterioration in the Quality of Foreign Bonds Issued in the United States, 1920–1930* (New York: National Bureau of Economic Research, 1951), p. 27.
[53] U.S. Department of Commerce, *Handbook on American Underwriting of Foreign Securities*, Trade Promotion Series, No. 104 (Washington, 1930), pp. 56–57.

48 1920's. Beyond that, probably little could be said. Specifically, they provide no indication on the truly interesting question: Could many more issues of the less-developed countries have been floated had the returns to investors been higher than they actually were? An econometric estimation of the demand function for less-developed countries' issues based on the meager data available would, of course, be absolutely out of the question.

LEGAL AND ADMINISTRATIVE HURDLES

Rules and regulations on public issuance of securities in the United States were greatly tightened in the 1930's, following the widespread bond defaults during the early part of the decade. Congressional hearings on the causes of the financial crisis revealed a great deal of laxity and sometimes unethical practices in the 1920's on the part of some investment bankers in pushing the sale of domestic and foreign bonds on a gullible and unprotected public.[54] To correct the laxity and prevent future malpractices in the securities markets, the Congress passed the Securities Act of 1933 and the Securities Exchange Act of 1934. The former requires the registration with the Securities and Exchange Commission of all *new issues,* domestic or foreign, floated publicly within the United States or its territories; the latter Act requires registration of, and periodic reporting on, *existing securities* widely held in the United States and traded in the U.S. securities markets. Both acts specify the kind of information that must be filed in the registration statements, and hold the security underwriters and the representatives of the borrowers

---

[54] For details, see *Hearings Before a Subcommittee of the Committee on Banking and Currency,* U.S. Senate, Pursuant to S. Res. 84, 72nd Congress, and S. Res. 56 and S. Res. 97, 73rd Congress (Washington, 1932 and 1933); *Hearings Before the Committee on Finance,* U.S. Senate, pursuant to S. Res. 19, 72nd Congress (Washington, 1932). Some of the highlights of these lengthy hearings have been summarized and analyzed in Mintz, *Deterioration in Quality of Foreign Bonds,* pp. 63–86, and in Madden *et al., America's Experience as a Creditor Nation,* pp. 204–31.

personally responsible for the authenticity and accuracy of the information, subject to both civil and criminal prosecutions.

In addition to Federal legislations, various states also have the so-called "Blue Sky laws,"[55] which require the registration with state commissions of any securities to be issued or sold in the respective states, as well as legal investment laws, which limit the types of securities which state-incorporated institutional investors—such as banks, insurance companies, trust funds, and investment funds—can purchase. The legal complexities are compounded by the fact that these statutes vary from state to state, and that separate proceedings for registration and qualification for legal investment must be instituted with the proper state authorities before a security can be sold in that state.

The upshot of all this is that issuing a security in the United States has become a highly complex technical operation, requiring the expert service of a battery of lawyers, accountants, and economists to provide and pore over a vast amount of statistical data needed for the satisfaction of all the legal requirements.[56] Whereas most of these requirements are no doubt needed for the protection of investors' interests, they could conceivably constitute "an appalling burden for poorer countries where the scarcity of statistical material is paralleled only by the even greater scarcity of trained personnel to process it."[57]

To what extent the less-developed countries have

[55] The name is reported to derive from a remark by one of the proponents of such laws that certain groups were trying to capitalize the blue sky. See Raymond E. Deely, "World Bank Bonds in the World's Capital Markets," *Finance and Development*, III, No. 3 (September 1966), 181.

[56] The staggering complexity of the statutory requirements and the literalism with which these requirements are interpreted are vividly described in Edward Nevins, "Some Reflections on the New York New Issue Market," *Oxford Economic Papers*, New Series, 13, No. 1 (February 1961), 84–102. For an account of the World Bank's experience in floating its first bond issues in the United States, see Deely, *World Bank Bonds*, p. 181.

[57] See Nevins, "Some Reflections on the New York New Issue Market," p. 102.

been hindered by these legal and administrative hurdles from issuing securities in the United States is difficult to determine. It may nevertheless be suggestive to note that, from 1958 to 1965, 15 less-developed countries succeeded in so doing, and they range from the Belgian Congo to Malaysia, Mexico, and Venezuela, differing widely in the degree of efficiency of their government apparatus and in the quality of their statistical reporting. Moreover, the U.S. securities market is well organized to provide the requisite expert services for security flotations in that market. With determination and perseverance, there is no reason for believing that the legal and administrative hurdles in the market should be insurmountable.

In concluding this lengthy section, a recapitulation of the analytical results seems to be called for. All the five popular explanations reviewed in this section are undoubtedly *relevant* factors in accounting for the failure of the less-developed countries to make effective use of international securities markets as a regular source of development capital. How *significant* each of these factors has been, however, is another matter.

Past debt defaults are relevant only insofar as they have adversely affected the general public's confidence in foreign bonds. However, investment in foreign securities is a sophisticated business and that the general public should shy away from it is not the least surprising. I found no evidence to suggest, however, that the professional institution investors, who are the pace setters in the market, are deterred by the debt defaults of the 1930's. Mexico's recent successes in floating bonds in the U.S. and European capital markets should be a clear indication that investors are more impressed with present capability and determination to service external debts than with what occurred more than a generation ago.

Political instability in a number of less-developed countries no doubt is an important factor in these countries' inability to sell bonds in international markets. However, the point would have to be stretched exceedingly thin before it could begin to cover most of the countries in Latin America, Asia, and North Africa. The fact that nearly all the less-developed countries have meticulously maintained full service on their postwar debts speaks well for their responsible attitudes towards meeting their external obligations.

The heavy debt burden some of the less-developed countries are already carrying may throw serious doubt on their capacity to incur additional debts through external bond issues. In many cases, however, the problem is largely one of poor maturity structure of debts. A restructuring of debts through bond issues would tend to lessen rather than enhance their debt burdens.

As to the costs of borrowing, it is true that the less-developed countries have had to pay considerably higher costs for bond issues in international markets than the developed countries. Yet, since the same countries have not seemed to eschew incurring huge amounts of short-term suppliers' credits often at relatively high interest costs, it is hard to conceive how borrowing costs could have been a significant deterrent to their issuing bonds in international markets.

Lastly, legal and administrative hurdles have been more a nuisance perhaps than a real barrier to the less-developed countries' bond issues in the United States, even though the same cannot be said of the situations in the European capital markets.

All in all, these popular explanations seem barely to have scratched the surface of the problem. By pooling them, one is still unable to state under what conditions a substantial revival of the international markets for the less-developed countries' bond issues could take place and could be sustained in the long run. To pursue an answer to that question, we can turn now to the next chapter.

CHAPTER FOUR

PROSPECTS FOR THE ISSUES IN INTERNATIONAL MARKETS

IN EVALUATING the prospect of re-vitalizing the international securities markets for less-developed countries' issues, it may be helpful to divide the discourse into two parts: the first, what is attainable within the present structure of the international securities markets, and the second, what fundamental weaknesses of the present structure must be overcome before a *sustainable* growth in less-developed countries' international issues could take place.

The present structure of international securities markets is characterized by laissez-faire-ism modified by government interventions for balance-of-payments purposes, for domestic economic policy purposes, and for the protection of investors against fraud or concealment of information.[58] According to this principle, risk-taking is re-

[58] The extent and means of government intervention differ greatly from one market to another. For a summary survey of conditions in European capital markets, see U.S. Department of Treasury, *A Description and Analysis of Certain European Capital Markets,* U.S. 88th Congress, Joint Economic Committee, Economic Policies and Practices Paper No. 3 (Washington, 1964), esp. pp. 33–44.

54   garded as the hallmark of private investment, and hence should be, and indeed is, left entirely to the investors, without any government assistance beyond the requirement of full and accurate disclosure of information relating to the issue by the prospective borrowers. In contrast to this hands-off policy towards risk-taking in foreign-securities investments, national governments and international agencies have in recent years increasingly veered towards a policy of risk-sharing with investors in such private ventures as direct investment in, and provision of suppliers' credit to, the less-developed countries.[59]

Can the volume of the less-developed countries' issues in international markets be substantially increased within the present structure of these markets?

As pointed out at the end of Chapter 2 (p. 26), in recent years the less-developed countries' issues in the U.S. market have expanded significantly in terms of not only the total volume of issues but also of the geographic dispersion of the issuers. For instance, the issues of the governments of Malaysia, Philippines, and Venezuela in 1965 were the first issues (other than those of U.S. direct-investment companies abroad) to be floated in the United States during the postwar period by less-developed countries outside the Central America and Caribbean regions. This broadening process continued in 1966 at a reduced rate and fell off sharply in 1967, presumably because of the unusually tight credit conditions in the United States. In the meantime, the rise of the Euro-dollar market has

[59] For a comprehensive and thorough study of U.S. Government programs in this area, see Marina von Neumann Whitman, *Government Risk-Sharing in Foreign Investment* (Princeton: Princeton University Press, 1966). For a study of national policies of export-credit insurance, see United Nations, Department of Economic and Social Affairs, *Export Credits and Development Financing* (New York, 1966), Parts I and II. Under the Auspices of the International Bank for Reconstruction and Development, an International Centre for Settlement of Investment Disputes was inaugurated in February 1967. For the basic document on it, see IBRD, *Convention on the Settlement of Investment Disputes Between States and Nationals of Other States,* report of the Executive Directors (Washington, March 18, 1965).

opened a great potential for the less-developed countries'
new issues.[60] In 1966, Gabon, Mexico, Peru, and Venezuela made Euro-dollar issues totaling $72 million.[61] These
developments lead one to believe that investors are certainly not unresponsive to the new issues of those less-
developed countries that exhibit convincing evidence of
stable and vigorous economic growth.[62]

However, it would be illusory to underestimate the
difficulty for a relatively new issuer from the less-developed countries to gain a firm foothold in international
capital markets. On that matter, Mexico's experience in
establishing itself as a regular borrower of good repute in
the U.S. and Euro-issue markets should be instructive.
Despite Mexico's political stability in the past half-century,
its rapid economic growth in the last 25 years, and its
monetary stability in the last decade, the markets did not
just "awake" by themselves to the attractiveness of Mexico's bond offerings. Instead, it took years of strenuous
effort on the part of both the Mexican Government and
the principal underwriters of its security issues to prepare
the ground, by calling the attention of American and
European investment institutions to the favorable conditions in Mexico.[63] Mexico's success may have some bene-
ficial "external effects" in paving the way for other less-
developed countries to issue securities in international

[60] The total size of the Euro-dollar pool has been estimated at between
$10 and $15 billion at the beginning of 1968. Long-term Euro-dollar loans
during the first ten days of 1968, following the announcement of the new
U.S. balance-of-payments program on January 1, 1968, exceeded the total
volume of such loans of $527 million in all 1967. See report by Tad Szulc
in *The New York Times,* February 1, 1968, pp. 49 and 54.

[61] See p. 26, n. 14.

[62] A partial list of such countries might be that presented by Mr.
George D. Woods, President of the World Bank, in his address to the
meeting of the Board of Governors in Rio de Janeiro on September 25,
1967: Iran, Israel, Korea, Malaysia, Mexico, Pakistan, the Republic of
China, Thailand, Tunisia, Venezuela, and Yugoslavia.

[63] In a letter to the author, Mr. Edgar R. Koerner of Kuhn, Loeb and
Co. of New York stated: "This educational process lasted over a period
of years, and, by the time we decided to make the first issue, potential
purchasers were quite familiar with Mexico." (Cited with permission.)

56   markets, insofar as suspicions and prejudices against these issues have thereby been reduced. However, by and large, each prospective issuing country will still have to plow its own ground, and the amount of preparatory work in each case should still be enormous.

The task has certainly not been made easier by the diverse, complex, and stringent investment and banking laws in various international capital markets, as pointed out earlier (pp. 48–50 and p. 49, n. 56). In this regard, the investment-banking industry in the developed countries could be of invaluable help to the less-developed countries by suggesting legislation to simplify legal requirements and procedures of security flotations in these markets without hamstringing national policies or weakening legitimate safeguards of investors' interests, and by establishing a machinery to provide technical assistance to the less-developed countries interested in issuing securities in international markets. The stigma of soliciting for business, which all reputable investment-bankers most assiduously seek to avoid, could be minimized if the technical-assistance program were to be run under the auspices of the entire industry, without partiality or prejudice to the interest of any individual firms in that industry.[64]

Perhaps, as in other areas of human endeavor, apathy and pessimism stemming from inertia, ignorance, or misunderstanding may have been important factors accounting for the small volume of the less-developed countries' issues in international capital markets. It is not inconceivable that, with a better understanding of the oppor-

[64] The Foreign Investment Committee, under the chairmanship of Arthur L. Wadsworth, of the Investment Bankers Association of America (IBA) did at one time take an active interest in providing assistance to the less-developed countries to gain access to the U.S. securities market. Its Washington subcommittee met in November 1960 and again in November 1961 with officials of international and U.S. Government agencies to explore ways of cooperation in this endeavor. For the subcommittee's reports on these meetings, see *The Commercial and Financial Chronicle* (New York), December 15, 1960, pp. 81ff., and December 28, 1961, p. 133. The subcommittee is now defunct. But, there is no reason why it cannot or should not be re-activated.

tunities open to them, the more favorably situated of these countries could be assisted to double or even triple their present volume of issues in international markets within two or three years after the program gets under way. In view of the small size of their present issues relative to the total magnitude of the markets, such an appraisal of the prospect might not be unduly optimistic.

Our interest, however, goes beyond the mere short-run prospect for the international issues of the more favorably situated less-developed countries. During most of the nineteenth century and the first decade of the twentieth century, the international securities market centered in London played a major role in development financing. Practically all the then developing nations were able to gain access to the market and they borrowed huge amounts of capital,[65] to the benefit of both the lending and the borrowing countries.[66] How likely is a restoration of that condition to take place within the present structure of international securities markets? What measures could be taken to help bring it about?

The world has of course changed greatly since the nineteenth century. For investors interested in foreign securities, perhaps the most significant change has been the much enhanced role of the government in the economic lives of all nations. This is especially so with respect to the issues of the less-developed countries. The upsurge of nationalism in these countries, the impact of

[65] Knowledge of international securities issues in the nineteenth century has been substantially advanced by a careful compilation of data on more than 41,000 foreign flotations in London during the period from 1865 to 1914. An analysis of these data by geographic distribution and type of issuer is presented in Matthew Simon, "The Pattern of New British Portfolio Foreign Investment, 1865–1914," in *Capital Movements and Economic Development,* edited by John H. Adler (New York: St. Martin's Press, 1967), pp. 33–60.

[66] Cairncross holds that nineteenth-century foreign investment yielded not only higher returns to British investors than home investment, but also contributed to the development of British export industry and reduction in the prices of imports. See Alexander K. Cairncross, *Home and Foreign Investment, 1870–1913* (Cambridge: Cambridge University Press, 1958).

58   the ideological split of the world into opposing camps, the predominant role of the governments in national economic development programs, and the overwhelming importance of public capital in the flow of financial resources to these countries have all contributed to rendering the prospect of these countries' ability and willingness to repay their foreign debts a function of decisions not only of the governments of these countries, but also of governments of the developed countries and of various public international agencies. Prospective investors are powerless to influence all these decisions and must find it exceedingly difficult to formulate predictions concerning them.

The primary difficulty in investing in foreign securities in general and in those of the less-developed countries in particular, therefore, lies not so much in the magnitude of the risks involved as in the *incalculability* of these risks from the viewpoint of the private investors. High risks could conceivably be compensated by high returns. It is when risks are of an incalculable sort that the price mechanism breaks down, as seems to have occurred since the Second World War in the international markets for the less-developed countries' securities issues.

Pursuing this line of thought further, one might ask the fundamental question: Why do investors tend to prefer domestic securities to foreign securities, and among the latter to prefer those of the developed countries to those of the less-developed countries—given the same degree of the liquidity of and familiarity with these securities, and aside from differences in the dependability of legal protection of contractual rights? A moment's reflection should lead one to the answer that the essential differences among these securities must lie in the severity of the "transfer problem" associated with the repayment of a debt, which means the problem of servicing a debt in the currency designated in the debt instrument, apart from the internal-solvency problem of the borrower. Thus defined, the transfer problem cannot arise at all with investment in domestic securities. And, at the international level, the severity of the problem depends on the type of international monetary system that prevails between the borrowing countries on one hand and the lending countries on the other.

A brief look into the history of international securities markets might help to make clear the significance of this point. Among the key factors accounting for the success of the London foreign-securities market as a major source of development financing in the nineteenth century is perhaps the unusually favorable international monetary condition then prevailing. Under the hegemony of the British pound, supported by the vast, unfettered international credit and capital market in London, and in the absence of independent national monetary management in the peripheral countries, a country's external-payments problem was then inseparable from the internal-solvency problem of the country's financial institutions,[67] and difficulties in servicing foreign debts were then largely those of the internal solvency of the individual borrowers. Under those conditions foreign issues flourished, because the risks in investing in foreign securities were essentially no different from those in domestic securities, except for legal protection of contractual rights under national courts and the extent of familiarity with the financial conditions of the borrowers, presumably both of which were adequately compensated for by higher returns on the investments.

The smooth functioning of the nineteenth-century international gold standard was shattered by World War

[67] For a similar view, see Walther Lederer, *The Balance of Foreign Transactions: Problems of Definition and Measurement,* Special Papers in International Economics, No. 5, International Finance Section, Princeton University (Princeton, 1963), pp. 5–12. Lederer states: "Provided, then, each layer of bank—from the local level through the various levels—makes sure to preserve its financial solvency, there is no difference between domestic and international solvency of the banking and currency systems." (Pp. 10–11.)

I, and after the war the center of international finance shifted from London to New York. The rise of the New York foreign-securities market in the 1920's coincided with a period of largely independent national efforts, with only limited inter-central bank cooperation,[68] to restore an international monetary system that was no more. The boom in that market proceeded with little public appreciation of the fundamental weaknesses of the international monetary condition then prevailing, and of the dependence of an international capital market on the smooth functioning of the underlying international monetary system. The precariousness of the market became obvious, belatedly, after its collapse and virtual demise in the early 1930's. For more than two decades thereafter, few foreign issues were floated in any international markets, aside from Canadian and World Bank issues in the United States.

The revival of foreign-securities markets in the 1950's, as noted in Chapter 2 (p. 18), was characterized by strict compartmentalization of the markets, so that an overwhelming portion of the foreign issues in each of the markets was floated by countries with which the market country had special financial ties. Although other factors —such as political considerations—undoubtedly were also at work, the compartmentalization of international securities markets in the 1950's seems to be another evidence lending at least partial support to the hypothesis relating the vitality of an international securities market to the viability of the international monetary condition underlying it.

An even more reassuring evidence is the fact that a revival of European issues in the United States did not get under way until after the external convertibility of European currencies in 1958. The gradual revival paral-

---

[68] For a lucid account of the major international monetary problems and the inter-central bank cooperations to cope with them during that period, see Stephen V. O. Clarke, *Central Bank Cooperation, 1924–31* (New York: Federal Reserve Bank of New York, 1967).

leled a process of progressive integration of the United States and European money markets through the interlacing of foreign-branch banking among these countries and through the mushrooming Euro-dollar market. Inexorably, threads were reaching out to weave together the heretofore largely independent national financial systems into a close-knit "trans-Atlantic financial community," which was broadened in the early 1960's to include Japan as well. These developments through private initiative have compelled the monetary authorities of the countries in this community to recognize that national economic policies have become matters of their common concern and that a financial crisis threatening one threatens them all. The institutions of monthly meetings at Basle of the central bankers of the Group-of-Ten countries, of regular meetings of the finance ministers of the member countries of the Organization for Economic Cooperation and Development and its various Working Parties, of intercentral bank swap arrangements, of the General Agreement to Borrow, and of the London Gold Pool are all reflections and outcomes of this official recognition. By the mid-1960's, then, a new international monetary order had emerged *among the developed nations,* which was akin in many respects to the nineteenth-century gold standard, except that the U.S. dollar had replaced the British pound as the major circulating international money, and a system of "multilateral surveillance" was being substituted for automatism in balance-of-payments adjustments.

As long as this emerging new international monetary order functioned smoothly so that the "transfer problems" among its member nations were effectively minimized, a basis existed for a sustained growth of foreign securities issues among the member nations, as did indeed take place with a tremendous upsurge of European and Japanese issues in the United States from 1958 to 1963. That official restrictive measures had to be applied to these issues in

July 1963 and have been maintained since merely reflects the fact that the "rules of the game" of this new international monetary order have not yet been worked out and are still a topic of intense discussion among the participating nations.[69] In the meantime, the rapid growth of the Euro-issue market is another indication that the forces pushing towards the formation of an "Atlantic capital market" have been relentlessly at work, despite all the official misgivings and active interventions.[70]

The future of the rising "Atlantic capital market" cannot be predicted at this point. But, one thing is clear: there has been a strong undercurrent sweeping towards the rise of an international capital market among the developed nations, and monetary authorities of these nations are kept busy attempting to cope with the payments-adjustment problems arising from the trend. Whether these problems are real or illusory is beside the point. The relevant observation here is that the rising international capital market among the developed nations is at once a symptom, a contributing factor, and an outcome of the emerging international monetary order among the developed nations, in which nearly all the less-developed countries are not now included.

The non-inclusion of the less-developed countries in the emerging international monetary order among the developed countries is, of course, not a matter of deliberate exclusion by the latter countries, but rather a reflection of the economic and financial conditions in the less-developed countries and a lack of policy coordination between the two groups of countries.

In the first place, the money and capital markets in most of the less-developed countries are still very rudi-

[69] See, e.g., Organization for Economic Cooperation and Development, *The Balance of Payments Adjustment Process,* a report by Working Party No. 3 of the OECD Economic Policy Committee (Paris, August 1966).
[70] For a similar view, see Charles P. Kindleberger, "European Economic Integration and the Development of a Single Financial Center for Long-Term Capital," *Weltwirtschaftliches Archiv,* 90, No. 2 (1963), 189–208. See also Peter B. Kenen, "Towards an Atlantic Capital Market," *Lloyds Bank Review,* No. 69 (July 1963), pp. 15–30.

mentary, largely as a result of which, and in many cases also because of exchange control regulations, both the assets and liabilities of banks, financial intermediaries, and other types of firms in these markets are almost completely local in nature, that is to say, having little marketability abroad. Hence, the impact of any temporary shortfalls in the economy's current foreign-exchange earnings relative to current expenditures receives little cushioning by appropriate adjustments in the portfolios of private individuals and institutions, but is directly transmitted to the official foreign reserves of the country.[71] The official reserves of most of the less-developed countries, in turn, are small relative to the amplitudes of fluctuations in the countries' current-account earnings and expenditures. Moreover, their official reserves are to a far less extent protected by such international credit facilities as are available to the official reserves of the developed nations.

In short, because of the lack of financial integration with markets abroad and because of the inadequate official reserves, the balances of payments of the less-developed countries are particularly vulnerable to occasional stresses, sometimes developing into crises, which threaten the countries' capacities to honor all their external obligations.

So far we have dealt only with the financial aspect of less-developed countries' balance-of-payments problems. In addition, there is the real aspect to consider. In many less-developed countries the balance of payments is in a state of what Kindleberger calls "secular disequilibrium" in the sense that there exists in these countries a tendency for domestic investments to outrun domestic savings to an

---

[71] The importance of internationally integrated financial markets in smoothing the balance-of-payments adjustment process has been stressed by James C. Ingram in his "State and Regional Payments Mechanism," *The Quarterly Review of Economics,* 73, No. 4 (November 1959), 619–32, and in his *Regional Payments Mechanisms: The Case of Puerto Rico* (Chapel Hill: The University of North Carolina Press, 1962). See also Tibor Scitovsky, "The Theory of Balance-of-Payments Adjustment," *Journal of Political Economy,* 75, No. 4, Supplement Part 2 (August 1967), 523–31, and comments by Haberler, Kenen, Cooper, and Mikesell in the same issue, 531–45.

64 extent exceeding the expected rate of capital inflows.[72] Given the rate of capital inflows, the problem has its roots in overambitious development programs, improper or ineffectual monetary and fiscal policies, and rigidities in the socio-economic structure of the country, such that real adjustments in its balance of payments are too little and too slow relative to the size of the country's official reserves.

The problem of insufficient real adjustments in the balance of payments is, of course, neither peculiar nor common to the less-developed countries. As pointed out earlier, it has been a matter of major concern among the developed nations too. The difference is that, whereas a start has been made among the developed nations to institute a system of "multilateral surveillance" in an attempt to work out mutually acceptable rules of behavior to bring about effective real adjustments, little headway has been made in this direction with regard to the less-developed countries beyond consultations between aid-receiving countries on the one hand and their major sources of external finance on the other, under arrangements such as aid consortia and consultative groups organized by the World Bank and Inter-American Development Bank.[73]

To say that the less-developed countries today are not included in, or at best are only on the fringe of, the emerging international monetary order among the developed nations is only a shorthand way of saying that the economic and financial links between the two groups of countries are not as conducive to minimization of the "transfer problem" between them as among the developed countries. Of the economic and financial links, we have identified two categories as of vital importance to the smooth functioning of an international monetary order: (1) ample provision of international liquidity either through inter-

[72] See Charles P. Kindleberger, *International Economics,* 3rd edition (Homewood, Ill.: Irwin, 1963), pp. 554–58.
[73] See United Nations, Department of Economic and Social Affairs, *World Economic Survey, 1965* (New York, 1966), pp. 131–38.

national integration of money and capital markets or through assured access to official sources of emergency credits or through both, and (2) harmonization of economic policies among the member countries of the community to permit and expedite real adjustments in order to eliminate persistent payments imbalances. It is worth re-emphasizing that the difference between the relative fulfillment of these conditions among the developed nations on one hand and the relative non-fulfillment with respect to the less-developed countries on the other is a matter of degree, not of kind.

Historically, as pointed out earlier, a smoothly functioning international monetary order seems to be a requisite of a vigorous and stable international securities market. Where the basic conditions are lacking, a boom in foreign securities might appear, with investors carried away by overoptimism and high returns of foreign securities, only to be confronted with defaults or near defaults during times of stress in the borrowing country's balance of payments. The ensuing frantic rush to dump these securities on a seemingly bottomless market and cessation of desperately needed capital flows to the borrowing country in question have worked havoc upon both the investors and the borrowers alike. Investors may or may not have learned their lesson. In either case, the stakes involving the stable growth of the world economy are just too high to leave to chance or to private risk-taking alone.

Effective policy measures ought to be devised and adopted to strengthen the economic and financial links between the less-developed countries on the one hand and the emerging international monetary order among the developed countries on the other, so that a secure foundation could be laid for a *sustainable* growth of the less-developed countries' issues in international markets. Short of that, much hope cannot be held for restoration of international new-issue markets to their former role as a major source of development finance.

CHAPTER FIVE

THE WORLD BANK AND THE LESS-DEVELOPED COUNTRIES' ISSUES IN INTERNATIONAL MARKETS

THE FOUNDING FATHERS of the Bretton Woods system foresaw the need for massive and energetic assistance by a public international agency to foster private capital flows to the war devastated and the less-developed countries in the postwar period.[74] The Articles of Agreement of the International Bank for Reconstruction and Development[75]

[74] In his opening speech introducing the proposal for an international bank for that purpose, Keynes stated at the Bretton Woods Conference in July 1944: "In the dangerous and precarious days which lie ahead, the risks of the lender will be inevitably large and most difficult to calculate. The risk premium reckoned on strict commercial principles may be beyond the capacity of an impoverished borrower to meet, and may itself contribute to the risks of ultimate default. Experience between the wars was not encouraging. Without some supporting guarantee, therefore, loans which are greatly in the interest of the whole world, and indeed essential for recovery, may prove impossible to float." See John Maynard Keynes, "The Bank for Reconstruction and Development," reprinted in *The New Economics*, edited by Seymour E. Harris (London, Dobson, 1948), p. 398.

[75] One of the names proposed and considered at the Bretton Woods Conference for the new bank was "The International Guarantee and Investment Association." See U.S. Department of State, *Proceedings and Documents of the United Nations Monetary and Financial Conference, Bretton Woods, New Hampshire, July 21–22, 1944* (Washington, 1948), 1, 366.

explicitly states that one of the purposes of the Bank is "to promote private foreign investment by means of guarantees or participations in loans and other investments made by private investors" (Article I). It even goes into considerable detail to stipulate the mode of operation regarding the type of private loans eligible for guarantees, the amount of guarantee commission to be charged by the Bank, and the provision of special reserve for meeting guarantee liabilities (Articles III and IV).

Paradoxically, throughout its more than two decades of operation, the Bank has never used this guarantee authority, except in the sale to private investors of seasoned loans from its own portfolio prior to mid-1956. A perusal of all the Bank's annual reports has turned up only a single reference to this failure to use its guarantee authority. In its *Tenth Annual Report, 1954–55,* p. 37, it is stated:

> The authors of the charter had believed that one of the new institution's chief means of performing its function would be to attach its guarantee to bond issues offered to private investors by its member countries. But when the Bank concluded that it would have to become an active lender itself, it had to decide also that it would itself become an active issuer in the capital market.

A fuller explanation was later given by the Bank in a review of its policies and operations published in 1957:

> At Bretton Woods it was believed that the guarantee of loans made by private investors would be the major function of the Bank. In practice, operations have not developed in that direction. There are a number of reasons for this. When the Bank started operations, its credit had not been established and it was likely that if it guaranteed any loans they would bear varying rates, influenced by the credit of the borrowers. Moreover, since securities guaranteed by the Bank would not have been as readily marketable as its direct obligations, use of the guarantee would have increased the cost of money to the borrowers. Consequently, it was decided to con-

centrate on selling the Bank's own bonds in the market, and to use the proceeds for direct loans.[76]

Both the validity and the relevance of the two reasons given—varying interest rates and higher interest cost—may be questioned. First, although the point about the Bank's credit position's not having been established was no doubt true with respect to the late 1940's, its continued validity in the 1950's is rather dubious. It seems unlikely that by the mid-1950's, Bank-guaranteed issues of different member countries would still have to bear varying interest rates despite the fact that they would all have been equally and fully backed by the resources at the Bank's disposal. Moreover, even if rates should have to be different according to the credit standing of the borrower, and even if the borrowers should have to pay higher costs than they would on the Bank's loans, it is not clear how that would have mattered to the borrowers in view of their acute need for external capital at all reasonable costs.

Although the Bank's explanation for not using the guarantee authority cannot be deemed satisfactory, the wisdom of the decision need not depend on its own explanation for it. The fact is, the Bank has done a superb job in generating private capital flows to its member countries without having to invoke the guarantee authority. Since 1947, it has floated about $5.5 billion of its own bonds in various capital markets;[77] in addition, the Bank has since 1948 sold more than $1 billion of seasoned loans from its own portfolio to private institutions, nearly all of which was without recourse to the Bank;[78] finally, it has also

[76] See the International Bank for Reconstruction and Development, *The World Bank: Policies and Operations* (Washington, 1957), p. 92.

[77] According to Raymond E. Deely, Chief of the Securities Division at the Bank, gross borrowings of the Bank totaled $4,970 million as of March 31, 1966. During the year ended June 30, 1967, gross borrowings amounted to another $554 million. See Deely, "World Bank Bonds in World's Capital Markets," *Finance and Development*, III, No. 3 (September 1966), 180, and the Banks' *Annual Report, 1966–67*, p. 3.

[78] Up-to-date data on the Bank's sale of seasoned loans are lacking. It is known that by mid-1956, when the Bank decided to cease providing

achieved signal successes in getting private institutions to participate in its loans to its member countries.[79] It might be argued that the Bank has found better ways to generate private capital flows to its member countries than through the use of its guarantee authority. In effect, the Bank has offered itself as a funnel for attracting and gathering private capital from all major international markets and distributing it to its member countries through its own loans.

The crucial question then becomes whether the Bank's loans to its member countries may be regarded as a perfect, or perhaps superior, substitute to providing guarantees to the latter's security issues in international markets. If the answer were negative, the proper course of action would be to take the Bank to task to explain more adequately than it has done why it has never used its guarantee authority and, short of a satisfactory explanation, to exert pressure on it to start using that authority. On the other hand, if the answer were positive, as I believe it should be, the Bank's policy of not using the authority would be vindicated, and one must then start looking for other ways to foster the growth of the less-developed countries' issues in international markets.

The key to the answer seems to lie in Article III, Section 4(vii) of the Bank's Articles of Agreement, which stipulates that "loans made or guaranteed by the Bank shall, except in special circumstances, be for the purpose of specific projects of reconstruction or development." In

---

guarantees to future loan sales, total sales had reached almost $280 million, of which over $200 million were without recourse to the Bank. By mid-1961, the total had exceeded $1 billion, amounting to nearly one-fifth of the Bank's loans to its member countries. See the Bank's *Sixteenth Annual Report, 1960–61*, pp. 7–9.

[79] Cumulative data on private participations in Bank loans are not available. An example of such joint operations may be cited for illustration. Together with a $7.7 million Bank loan to Zambia and Rhodesia in October 1964 for development of electric power, a group of ten U.S. and European banks extended loans totaling $4.5 million in the same project. See the Bank's *Annual Report, 1964–65*, p. 69.

fact, the Bank's lending operations have been very much within the confines of this provision. As of mid-1967, out of a total of more than $12 billion in loans it had made, only about $200 million was listed as "general development" loans, the rest being all for "specific projects."[80] As long as this provision stands, it should make little difference to the prospective borrower whether a "specific project" approved by the Bank was to be financed by a direct loan from the Bank or by the proceeds from selling its own securities guaranteed by the Bank. If anything, the former should be the far simpler method, in view of the awesome amount of work involved for meeting all the rules and regulations of issuing securities in international markets. From the Bank's point of view, as long as it is able to borrow a sufficient amount of private capital for relending, it should make more sense to follow the well-established procedure of administering its own loans than to venture into the unchartered territory of issuing bond guarantees, especially when the latter method cannot be expected to accomplish more than the Bank has achieved already.

In short, as long as the Bank guarantees can be issued only on bonds for the financing of "specific projects," the guarantee authority is an unnecessary duplication of the Bank's power to borrow on its own and use the proceeds to make loans for the same purpose. But, surely, the less-developed countries have many needs for foreign capital other than the financing of specific development projects. The Bank itself has long recognized the need for "program aid" in conjunction with "project aid,"[81] and in its operations organized numerous aid consortia and consultative groups together with other aid-giving agencies to appraise

[80] See the Bank's *Annual Report, 1966–67*, p. 66.
[81] There has been a recent revival of interest in the old controversy over the relative merits of "project aid" versus "program aid." The former may be defined, to use Alan Carlin's definitions, as "assistance whose disbursement is tied to capital investment in a separable productive

the overall foreign-assistance needs of individual less-developed countries, thereby helping the latter to arrange for non-project aids from other sources.[82]

In fact, the more favorably situated of the less-developed countries have used the proceeds of their international bond issues for the refunding of their external debts and other general development purposes.[83] Like a business firm situated in a country with a well-developed capital market, a few of these countries have been able to make good use of the financial flexibility accorded them by virtue of their ready access to assured external borrowings, in their planning for economic growth. Unfortunately, this option is not open to the majority of the less-developed countries. Without massive assistance by a public international agency such as the World Bank, they have not been able to float securities in international markets, as the founding fathers of the Bretton Woods institutions had accurately anticipated.

Amending the Bank's Articles of Agreement so as to permit it to guarantee bond issues for general development purposes might appear to be a possible solution, but in all

activity," and the latter as "assistance whose disbursement is tied to the recipient's expenditures on a wide variety of items justified in terms of the total needs and development plan of the country rather than any particular project." See Alan Carlin, "Project Versus Programme Aid: From the Donor's Viewpoint," *The Economic Journal,* No. 305 (March 1967), p. 49. See also Hans W. Singer, "External Aid: For Plans or Projects," *The Economic Journal,* No. 299 (September 1965), pp. 539–45.

[82] The U.S. foreign economic aid about 1964, for instance, was nearly equally divided between program and project assistance. See U.S. Agency for International Development, Program Coordination Staff, *Principles of Foreign Economic Assistance* (Washington, 1964), p. 34.

[83] A typical statement of the purpose of the Government of Mexico's issues in the United States describes the intended use of the loan proceeds as follows: "The proceeds of the bonds will be applied by the Government to foreign exchange expenditures required for the purchase of capital equipment in conjunction with certain of its economic development projects . . . or to the refunding of its outstanding indebtedness held by financial institutions abroad, principally in the United States, which was originally incurred to help finance economic development projects." See *Prospectus,* Mexico 6.25 percent external sinking fund bonds due November 1, 1979, dated October 27, 1964 (New York: Kuhn, Loeb and Co., 1964), p. 4.

likelihood seems to be neither politically feasible nor necessarily desirable. In view of the present diverse opinions on the relative desirability of "program aid" versus "project aid," there is serious doubt if such a proposal could ever muster sufficient support in the Bank's Board of Executive Directors, not to mention the difficulty in getting ratification by three-fifths of the Bank's members having four-fifths of the total voting power, as required for any amendment of the Bank's Articles of Agreement. Moreover, as pointed out earlier, providing full guarantee of a borrower's debt is in essence no different from incurring a direct debt of one's own and then relending the proceeds to the ultimate borrower. If ever an amendment of the Bank's Articles of Agreement were to come about to extend its scope of operation to include loans and guarantees for general development purposes, it would only be natural and reasonable to expect the Bank to have a predilection for using the tested loan technique of more than 20 years' standing over the unfamiliar guarantee technique; in short, the guarantee authority would still lie unused.

In essence, to regard a Bank guarantee as a necessary condition for successful flotations of the less-developed countries' international issues is a defeatist attitude, justifiable only at a time when there was no hope of eradicating the root of the problem. The Bank-guarantee scheme was intended to treat only the symptoms, not the causes, of the collapse of international markets for less-developed countries' issues, and hence at best could only provide temporary relief to the problem. As temporary reliefs go, the guarantee might have to be relied on indefinitely without significant improvement in the basic conditions, and the Bank might therefore from time to time end up holding the bag in case of default resulting from serious deteriorations in the basic conditions underlying the international securities markets.

74   World conditions have changed much since 1944. It is doubtful if the founding fathers of the Bretton Woods system would still advocate a Bank-guarantee scheme under the conditions of the world today. What would have been utterly impracticable about a quarter of a century ago has now come within reach. Perhaps the time has arrived to start devising a scheme that would eradicate the root of the problem, rather than merely treating its symptoms.

CHAPTER SIX

WORLD BANK CERTIFICATION
OF THE ISSUES

THE FAILURE of international security markets to resume their former role as a major source of development finance has been attributed in Chapter 4 to two basic factors: (1) Incalculability of risks in investment in less-developed countries' securities, because of the high degree of dependence of these countries' debt-servicing capacities on government policies in these countries on the one hand and on the policy decisions of the developed nations and of various public international agencies on the other; and (2) the lack of a smoothly functioning international monetary order linking the less-developed countries with the developed countries that would reduce to a minimum the "transfer problem" between them. Essential conditions for such an international monetary order include (a) ample provision of international liquidity to absorb temporary shocks to external-payments positions, and (b) harmonization of economic policies for effective real adjust-

76 ments to take place for the elimination of persistent payments imbalances.

These are indeed formidable obstacles to the less-
developed countries' issues in international markets and
appear to account for much of the profound inactivity of
these issues in the last forty years. Unless effective measures
are taken for their removal, there may be little hope for a
sustained revival of the international securities markets for
development financing. But that is no ground for pessimism. On the contrary, an understanding of the nature
of these obstacles helps to lay the basis for proposing
appropriate measures for their removal. Moreover, there
are reasons to believe that these measures are by no means
out of reach, and that the time is now ripe to give serious
consideration to the possible adoption of these measures.

In a nutshell, what I propose is a scheme calling for
the World Bank to undertake certification of less-developed countries' bond issues in international markets, upon
the borrowing country's request and upon satisfaction of a
number of conditions to be specified below. A "World
Bank certification" would be an official proclamation by
the Bank that it has examined and found satisfactory the
borrower's ability to service the new debt in accordance
with terms set forth in the bond issue, and that the Bank
further commits itself to take an active interest in the
continued observance of these terms throughout the life
of the issue.

The issuance of such a certification might be predi-
cated on the satisfaction of the following conditions:

(1) That the issue to be certified be a direct obliga-
tion of a member of the World Bank or fully guaranteed
by the member or the central bank or some comparable
agency of the member which is acceptable to the Bank;

(2) That the member demonstrate to the Bank's satisfaction that the net proceeds from the proposed issue

should make a significant contribution to the long-run economic development of the country, and that its servicing would not be an unsupportable burden on the country's external-payments position;

(3) That the member agree to periodical reviews with the Bank of the country's external-payments position and to adopt suitable policies worked out in conjunction with the Bank for the elimination of any persistent imbalance in its payments position; and

(4) That the member be a Contracting State of the Convention on the Settlement of Investment Disputes and duly notify the International Centre for Settlement of Investment Disputes that it considers disputes over the Bank-Certified bonds as under the jurisdiction of the Centre in accordance with Article 25(4) of the said Convention.

Condition (1) needs little explanation. It delimits the bond issues eligible for Bank certification to those that would be eligible for Bank guarantees according to Article III, Section 4 of the Bank's Articles of Agreement. The reason for the delimitation is simple. The Bank certification imposes a number of obligations on the central government of the borrowing country, as specified in conditions (2) to (4). Hence, unless the central government is directly involved in the bond issue either as the borrower or as a full guarantor, it would make no sense to require it to assume those obligations, nor would the government likely consent to do so unless it is thus involved.

Condition (2) requires the member applying for Bank certification of bond issues to enter into an understanding with the Bank on its development program, including a projection of its balance of payments, over a sufficiently long period (say, three to five years), as well as on an outline of the policies through which the goals of the development program and of the balance of payments are to be

78 implemented. The condition is essentially the same as that which the Bank has consistently applied ever since the start of its operations in its investigations prior to the granting of a loan.[84] Not infrequently, the Bank has required, as a condition for granting a loan, changes in the borrowing country's economic policies in order to ensure stable growth of the country's economy and the repayment prospect of the Bank loan.[85]

The Bank has produced studies on the economic positions and prospects of some ninety-five countries and territories, and from time to time sent review missions to these countries to bring the studies up to date.[86] In recent years, it has also established, in cooperation with the OECD, a new expanded system of reporting external debts and international capital flows.[87] Perhaps, more than any other institution, it is in possession of the most comprehensive, reliable, and up-to-date information on the economic conditions and external-debt problems of its member countries. All that fountain of knowledge plus its incomparable experience in evaluating the long-run economic prospects of its member countries could be put to use for assisting private investors' appraisal of the creditworthiness of less-developed countries' issues.

Condition (3) requires periodical reviews of the economic condition and policies of the borrowing country subsequent to the certification and throughout the life of the issue. Again, the condition does not represent a drastic departure from the Bank's long standing practices. As a part of its ongoing policy, the Bank keeps abreast of

[84] The pre-investment investigation process has included "a general examination of the economy of the borrowing country with a view to determining (1) the approximate amount of additional external debt the country can afford to service and the rate at which it can effectively absorb such debt, . . . and (3) the appropriateness of the government's economic and financial policies to further the development process." See the International Bank for Reconstruction and Development, *Fifth Annual Report, 1949–50*, pp. 11–13.

[85] *Ibid.*

[86] See IBRD, *Annual Report, 1964–65*, p. 10.

[87] See IBRD, *Annual Report, 1966–67*, p. 16.

the developments in the borrowing country's economic position and, when deemed necessary, suggests what it regards as suitable policy changes in order to ensure the country's continued ability to service the Bank's loans.[88] Under the scheme being proposed here, some formal procedure might be worked out to require annual position reviews, similar to the annual consultations with the International Monetary Fund of those Fund members retaining exchange restrictions under Article XIV, Section 2, of the Fund Agreement.[89] In consonance with established practice, reports of such consultations should not be published. Holders of the Bank-certified bonds, nevertheless, could take comfort in the assurance that the Bank remains vigilant to developments in the borrowing country to ensure the latter's continued capability to service the bonds.

Condition (4) requires a commitment on the borrower's part to consider submitting to conciliation or arbitration any disputes arising between itself and the holders of the Bank-certified bonds in accordance with the provisions of the Convention on the Settlement of Investment Disputes Between States and Nationals of Other States.[90] Applied to the scheme under consideration, the Convention would bring about quite an innovation in the international securities market, even though, should the scheme work out smoothly, the procedures established under the convention would never need to be resorted to.

[88] See IBRD, *Fifth Annual Report, 1949–50,* pp. 16–17.

[89] In view of the proliferation of similar periodical consultations, there is much to be said for effecting some coordination among the national and international agencies conducting such consultations in order to avoid unnecessary duplications and lessen their burden on the less-developed countries. I am grateful to John H. Adler, Senior Adviser of the IBRD, for pointing this out to me.

[90] The Convention, formulated by the Executive Directors of the World Bank and submitted to members of the Bank for signature and ratification, came into force on October 14, 1966, 30 days after the deposit of the twentieth instrument of ratification. By August 1, 1967, it had been signed by 35 countries and ratified by 32. See IBRD, *Annual Report, 1966–67,* p. 20.

The fact is, investment in foreign securities has always been regarded as purely private risk-taking, improper for governments to become involved in, except to the extent of compelling disclosure of information relating to the issue and extending protection of contractual rights within the jurisdictions of the national courts. In case of default by a borrower which is the government or a public agency of a foreign country, private investors are totally without legal resorts according to the doctrine of sovereign immunity,[91] and seldom do governments intervene in such cases on behalf of their own nationals. In the past, private organizations, such as the Foreign Bondholders Protective Council and the International Committee of Bankers on Mexico, have been established to represent investors in debt-settlement negotiations with defaulting foreign governments. But, even in cases where the foreign governments were willing to negotiate, the bargaining has always been one-sided insofar as the representatives of private investors have had little to rely on besides the good will and regard for its good reputation of the foreign government. Often, the representatives have had to accept whatever they could get under the circumstances; and, where the terms of settlement offers were found by the representatives to be unacceptable, private investors were left to decide on their own whether to accede to the unilateral offers of the foreign governments or to go completely without any payment of interest and principal on their investment.

As long as the doctrine of sovereign immunity stands, as it does today, fundamental changes in this situation are out of the question. The best one can hope for under the circumstances is an amelioration of the situation by making available a legal framework and apparatus for settling

[91] For a thorough and illuminating survey of the issues involved in the application of the doctrine, see Richard B. Lillich, *The Protection of Foreign Investment* (Syracuse: Syracuse University Press, 1965), esp. pp. 3–44.

CHAPTER SIX ● WORLD BANK CERTIFICATION OF THE ISSUES

disputes where both parties—governments and nationals
of other states—agree to conciliation or arbitration, such
as is provided in the Convention on the Settlement of
Disputes Between States and Nationals of Other States.
Thus, condition (4) requiring the borrowing country to
notify the International Centre for Settlement of Investment Disputes that it would consider submitting to the
jurisdiction of the Centre any disputes arising out of the
Bank-certified bonds, does in no way bind the borrowing
country to settle all such future disputes through the
Centre. The wording of Article 25(4) of the Convention
on this point is clear. Specifically, it states: "Such notification shall not constitute the consent required by paragraph (1)," and paragraph (1) of the same Article requires
written consents by the parties of a particular dispute to
submit the dispute to the Centre. In other words, the
notification under Article 25 (4) refers to a *class* of disputes which the Contracting State would *consider* submitting to the Centre, but the actual act of submitting a
specific dispute to the Centre requires written consents
from all parties to the dispute as the occasion arises.[92]

Moreover, even in the case where a State has given
consent to arbitration by the Centre, and the Centre's
arbitration awards are considered by all signatory States
of the Convention as binding (Article 53), the enforce-

[92] It may be worthwhile to cite the text of the two paragraphs in full.
Article 25(4) stipulates: "Any Contracting State may, at the time of ratification, acceptance or approval of this Convention or at any time thereafter, notify the Centre of the class or classes of disputes which it would
or would not consider submitting to the jurisdiction of the Centre. The
Secretary-General shall forthwith transmit such notification to all Contracting States. Such notification shall not constitute the consent required
by paragraph (1)." Article 25(1) states: "The jurisdiction of the Centre
shall extend to any legal dispute arising directly out of an investment,
between a Contracting State (or any constituent subdivision or agency of a
Contracting State designated to the Centre by that State) and a national
of another Contracting State, which the parties to the dispute consent in
writing to submit to the Centre. When the parties have given their consent, no party may withdraw its consent unilaterally." See IBRD, *Convention on the Settlement of Investment Disputes Between States and Nationals of Other States* (Washington, 1965), pp. 9–10.

82 ment of the awards is still subject to the laws of the State
in whose territories the enforcement is sought (Article 54),
specifically not to derogate from any law "relating to immunity of that State or of any foreign State from execution" (Article 55).

Clearly, then, the Convention offers little protection
against *arbitrary* and *willful* default by a borrowing country. Nevertheless, it represents an important step forward
for the protection of private foreign investors in that for
the first time a disinterested third party of great prestige
could be brought into a dispute over foreign investment,
for conciliation or arbitration according to prescribed
procedures, when both parties are willing to seek a settlement. Moreover, the stigma arising out of a refusal to
settle a legitimate claim after prior notification of readiness to consider submission to the Centre's procedures
should be so damaging to the country's repute that such
a course of action might be contemplated by a borrowing
country only in the most extreme circumstances.

The pre-certification investigation and subsequent
policy reviews stipulated in conditions (2) and (3) are
intended to help reduce the incalculability of risks from
the private investors' point of view of investing in the
less-developed countries' securities. Nevertheless, despite
utmost caution and diligence in their execution, occasions
might arise when insupportable strains develop in a borrowing country's balance of payments to jeopardize its
continued capability to service its external debts in full.
Such occasions might come about as a result of, for instance, crop failures, or unexpected declines in world
demand for the country's principal export commodities,
or civil disturbances disrupting or crippling production
and distribution in the country. For one reason or another,
as pointed out earlier (p. 37), a number of countries had
to request resettlement or re-scheduling of their external
debts during the 1960's, causing grave concern in the

minds of their creditors and likely also discouraging potential private capital inflows which were particularly needed during such times.

To assist its members experiencing temporary shortfalls in export earnings to avert balance-of-payments crises, the International Monetary Fund has had in operation since 1963 a scheme whereby such members are eligible for special drawings from the Fund to the full extent of the shortfall up to 25 percent of their respective quotas in the Fund.[93]

More recently, the World Bank staff has worked out, at the request of the First United Nations Conference on Trade and Development (UNCTAD), a scheme of Supplementary Financial Measures for providing long-term credits to less-developed countries confronted with unexpected shortfalls in export earnings, so as to enable them to avoid disruptions in their development programs.[94] As a condition for eligibility to such assistance, the Bank scheme requires that the participating less-developed countries reach prior understandings with the Bank on their development programs and agree to periodical reviews similar to those required in the scheme proposed in this study.

The Bank scheme has been under active consideration by the UNCTAD Committee on Invisibles and Financing Related to Trade.[95] Should it be accepted and the requisite amount of initial capital subscribed to by developed countries for it to start operation, it would be an invaluable complement to the Fund scheme, and the two together would virtually assure the participating less-developed countries ample credits to tide them over unexpected strains in their balance of payments.

The two principal features of the Bank scheme, policy

[93] See International Monetary Fund, *Compensatory Financing of Export Fluctuations* (Washington, first report, February 1963; second report, September 1966).

[94] See IBRD, *Supplementary Financial Measures* (Washington, December 1965).

[95] See IBRD, *Annual Report, 1966–67*, p. 17.

consultations and provision of supplementary liquidity, are precisely what have been referred to earlier in this study as characteristic of the new international monetary order that has been emerging among the developed countries since the late 1950's. If adopted and successfully operated, the scheme would in effect link the participating less-developed countries to the emerging monetary order among the developed countries, so that the "transfer problem" existing between the two groups of countries would largely be obliterated. A secure basis would then exist for a sustainable growth of the less-developed countries' securities in international markets, as has been maintained in Chapter 4.

Much, therefore, depends on the adoption and coming into force of the Bank's Supplementary Financial Measures scheme. If and when it does become a reality, the Bank-certification scheme proposed in this chapter can then be simply appended to it. However, should the Bank scheme fall through for lack of capital subscription, an alternative approach must be sought to provide the supplementary credits that will be needed to safeguard a borrowing country's debt-servicing capacity during times of unexpected stress.

A possibility might be the consultative-group approach for rendering and coordinating aid to less-developed countries. In the last decade the number of national and international agencies providing financial aid to the less-developed countries has grown rapidly,[96] and the need for achieving effective and purposeful coordination among them has long been recognized. The OECD Development Assistance Committee, for instance, was formed in 1960 to provide a forum for suppliers of bilateral assistance to less-developed countries to get together and exchange

[96] For a chronological listing of such international agencies that came into being from 1943 through 1966, see United Nations, Department of Economic and Social Affairs, *World Economic Survey, 1965* (New York, 1966), pp. 125–27.

experience on common problems.[97] More important as action groups are the various aid consortia and consultative groups organized by the World Bank and the Inter-American Development Bank for coordinating financial assistance to individual less-developed countries. Outstanding examples are the aid consortium for India formed in 1958, that for Pakistan in 1960, and the aid consultative groups since 1962 for Colombia, Ecuador, Malaysia, Nigeria, Sudan, Thailand, and Tunisia. The various consortia and consultative groups differ in composition of aid-giving countries as well as in mode of operation,[98] but they are all designed to extend coordinated assistance to an individual less-developed country through policy consultations and through the provision of development, as well as supplementary, financing.

In case the Supplementary Financial Measures scheme should fall through, some form of international coordination of aid ought to be incorporated into the Bank-certification scheme proposed here so that the existing aid consortia and consultative groups could be used, and new groups formed, to lend assurance of continuing interest and financial assistance to development efforts in the prospective borrowing country whose international bond issues were to be certified by the World Bank. The Bank, as the administering agency, would be responsible for conducting the periodical policy consultations and for convening the consultative group in case of need to de-

[97] The Committee now consists of 15 developed countries plus the Commission of the European Economic Community, and is one of the specialized Committees of the Organization for Economic Cooperation and Development. The annual reports of the Chairman of the Committee are published by the OECD under the title: *Development Assistance Efforts and Policies.*

[98] Aid consortia require explicit development programs and close surveillance of their execution; aid-giving participants in the consortia are expected to give pledges of specific amounts of funds. Consultative groups, in contrast, are much more informal and less binding in both policy surveillance and fund pledges. For an excellent survey of both types of international coordination of aid, see U.N., *World Economic Survey, 1965,* pp. 131–38.

termine the extent of financial assistance to be rendered to the less-developed country in question, just as it has been doing with the various existing aid consortia and consultative groups. The only difference under the scheme proposed here would be for the Bank to proclaim, on behalf of a consultative group at the time of its certification of an issue, the group's readiness to assist the issuing country in meeting its external obligations during times of unexpected stress.[99]

The above measures may be regarded as constituting the *core* of the Bank-certification scheme proposed in this study. In summary, the principal elements of the scheme consist of the following:

(1) *Pre-certification investigation* to ascertain the borrowing country's capability to service the additional debt;

(2) *subsequent periodical consultations* to assure continued creditworthiness of the debtor country;

(3) *possible resort* to the International Centre for Settlement of Investment Disputes in the event of a dispute; and

(4) *supplementary financing* under the Bank's Supplementary Financial Measures scheme and the International Monetary Fund's Compensatory Financing scheme in case of unexpected payments stress; or

(4a) *a consultative group* of capital-exporting nations to pledge assistance during times of payments stress.

The scheme should provide a secure basis for helping to bring about a revival of the international market for less-

[99] The precise terms of the proclamation need to be more clearly spelled out. It is possible that the group might indicate a special interest in assuring the servicing of the Bank-certified bond issue in question, to the extent of committing each of the participating aid-giving countries to provide "tied credit" to the borrowing country in an amount equivalent to the service payments due to those holders of the bond who are nationals of the aid-giving country. The payments could be made directly to the nationals of the aid-giving countries, thus by-passing the borrowing

developed countries' issues so that it may resume its former role as a major source of development finance.

Additional provisions may be added to facilitate the operation of the scheme. One such possibility would be for the Bank to apply to national and state authorities of major capital-exporting nations to recognize the Bank-certified bonds as legal instruments of investment, to be treated on the same basis as the Bank's own bonds. Another possibility would be the establishment of a special counter-speculative fund either within the Bank or separate from but operated by it for the stabilization of the market prices of Bank-certified bonds to keep their yields in line with market conditions. Successful open-market operation of such a fund would add significantly to the attractiveness of the Bank-certified bonds.[100] Lastly, some sort of adjustment assistance might be made available to capital-exporting countries whose balance-of-payments position might in the short run be adversely affected by its nationals' purchases of the Bank-certified bonds. This should not be a serious problem before the less-developed countries' issues had attained volume. But, eventually, if the scheme were successful, some adjustment assistance might become desirable or even necessary. Possible means might include special bond issues of the governments of the capital-exporting nations in temporary payments deficit up to amounts equivalent to the total volumes of the purchases of Bank-certified bonds by their nationals during the preceding year, to mature serially over a period of, say, five years, and to carry an interest

country and in effect giving priority to the servicing of the Bank-certified bonds, while not violating any pledge the borrowing country might have made to give most-favored treatment to its other types of external debts.

[100] It is conceivable that the International Monetary Fund, rather than the IBRD, should be asked to operate such a fund, using national currencies acquired by the Fund from cashing Special Drawing Rights especially allotted to it for the operation of the counter-speculative fund. That, of course, would require an amendment of the SDR scheme now being submitted to governments for ratification.

rate not lower than the highest yield on the Bank-certified bonds. Such special bonds could be subscribed to by the other capital-exporting nations according to some pre-arranged formula, or by the International Monetary Fund with national currencies purchased by it with Special Drawing Rights allotted to it for that purpose.

In conclusion, it should be emphasized that the scheme proposed in this study is not intended to replace any existing or proposed schemes for channeling financial resources to the less-developed countries. Indeed, as indicated above, the successful operation of the scheme would depend to a considerable extent on the continued and perhaps increased availability of public funds to assist less-developed countries in their development effort and in servicing a growing volume of external debts. In this connection, I have in mind especially the Horowitz Proposal, which suggests the establishment of an Interest Equalization Fund for absorbing the interest differentials between the rates paid by the World Bank for funds raised in capital markets and transferred at cost to the International Development Association and the rates received by the latter in relending the proceeds to the less-developed countries.[101] Surely, a multi-pronged approach toward mobilizing private capital for development financing could achieve results, through complementarity of the various individual schemes, far greater than the totality of their results when the effectiveness of each individual scheme is considered separately.

[101] The proposal was originally submitted by David Horowitz, Governor of the Bank of Israel, to the First United Nations Conference on Trade and Development in April 1964. See UNCTAD Document E/CONF.46/C.3/2. The document and subsequent statements and reports by Governor Horowitz, the IBRD staff, and a group of experts especially appointed by the Secretary General of the UNCTAD to study the proposal have been collected in *The Horowitz Proposal, Selected Documents,* third edition, 1966, made available to me through the courtesy of Mr. Guy F. Erb of the UNCTAD office in New York.

CHAPTER SIX ● WORLD BANK CERTIFICATION OF THE ISSUES

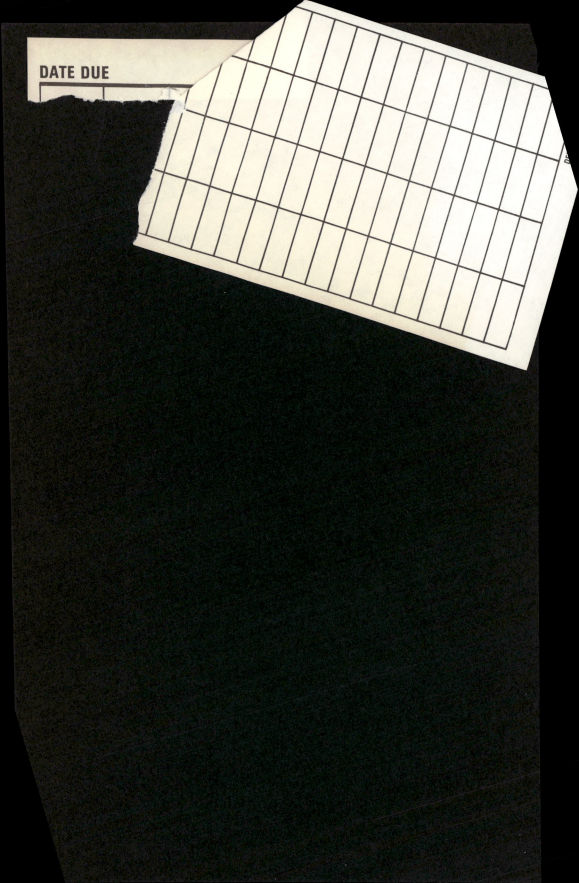